pd dup)

On Earth
as it is in Heaven

Josephine Lombardi

On Earth as it is in Heaven

NOVALIS

© 2010 Novalis Publishing Inc.

Cover design: Blaine Herrmann
Layout: Audrey Wells

Published by Novalis

Publishing Office
10 Lower Spadina Avenue, Suite 400
Toronto, Ontario, Canada
M5V 2Z2

Head Office
4475 Frontenac Street
Montréal, Québec, Canada
H2H 2S2

www.novalis.ca

Cataloguing in Publication is available from Library and Archives Canada.

Printed in Canada.

Some of the material of this book has been reworked from the author's doctoral dissertation, "The Universal Salvific Will of God in Official Documents of the Roman Catholic Church," published in 2007 by the Edwin Mellen Press. The material has been used with the kind permission of the Edwin Mellen Press, Lewiston, New York.

The Scripture quotations contained herein are from the New Revised Standard Version of the Bible, copyrighted 1989 by the Division of Christian Education of the National Council of the Churches of Christ in the United States of America, and are used by permission. All rights reserved.

We acknowledge the financial support of the Government of Canada through the Canada Book Fund for business development activities.

9 8 7 6 5   20 19 18 17 16

Contents

Foreword

During Jesus' earthly ministry we hear that a disciple asked him, "Lord, teach us to pray, as John taught his disciples" (Luke 11:1). Jesus' response to this request gave us the gift of the Lord's Prayer.

When we think about Luke's account of Jesus presenting the Lord's Prayer, we can relate to the disciple who wants some direction for how to pray. In times of struggle or joy, we may find it difficult to put our feelings into words. We want to talk to God, but may not know how to begin. Is prayer simply asking for something? Is prayer thanking God? Is prayer praising God? The answer to these questions can be found in the wonderful model for prayer that Jesus gave us.

This book shows us how the Lord's Prayer can help us when we want to talk to God. The author offers a reflection on the Lord's Prayer and relates each of the seven petitions to the concerns of everyday life. Drawing on her personal, professional, and academic experience, she proposes the idea that salvation is the fulfillment of the Lord's Prayer in our daily lives and in the world to come. By leading us through the pastoral, psychological, and spiritual insights revealed in each petition, Josephine affirms the universal and timeless importance of this prayer.

Catholics are a Eucharistic people. The Eucharist is the source and summit of the life of the Church and its greatest prayer. In the celebration of the Eucharist, therefore, we find the Lord's Prayer. Immediately after this prayer we have the Embolism (from the Greek word *embolisma,* meaning a patch or something added). As the Lord's Prayer ends with "but deliver us from evil," the embolism prayer continues, "Deliver us, Lord, from every evil, and grant us peace in our day … as we wait in joyful hope for the coming of our saviour, Jesus Christ." The Liturgy of the Church reminds us that the ultimate fulfillment of the Lord's Prayer is not only in this life, but also in the life to come, a fact that is clearly presented in this book.

As a married mother of four, Dr. Josephine Lombardi has served as a parish minister, campus minister, high school chaplaincy leader, and theologian. She uses her rich experience to encourage us to reconsider the everyday implications of the Lord's Prayer in our present needs and challenges. People of faith will find that her book affirms the depth and beauty of this ancient prayer. I encourage those who want to deepen their understanding of prayer to use this book as part of their spiritual reflection.

Jesus has given us a great gift in this prayer. As our Lord and Saviour, he affirms the need to pray always and shows us that God is concerned with all aspect of our lives. May *On Earth as it is in Heaven* help all of us draw closer to the Lord and live in joyful hope as we await his return.

Most Rev. Gerard Bergie
Auxiliary Bishop of Hamilton

Preface

My doctoral dissertation addressed God's will to save all people, not just baptized Christians. I showed how this mystery was understood throughout our Christian history and provided some commentary on where to go with the findings. The date selected for the defense—October 5, 2005—was connected to two special aspects of my study of salvation, which took me over ten years: mercy, and the Lord's Prayer. October 5 is the feast day of Saint Faustina Kawalska, the messenger of God's endless mercy. Also, that day, Luke's account of the Lord's Prayer was the gospel reading.

I am not a statistician, but I knew the odds were slim that I would defend my dissertation on a day that the Lord's Prayer was part of the daily Mass readings. Weekday Masses follow a two-year cycle that leads us through the scriptures. The Lord's Prayer appears only in Matthew's and Luke's gospels, further reducing the chances that this would be the gospel reading for that particular day. Was this a coincidence, or was it God's way of confirming the insights I gained during my decade-long search for the deeper meaning of salvation? I leave it to the reader to discern.

In the days leading up to my defense, I was very nervous. Arriving an hour early at the University of St. Michael's College, Toronto, where the defense would take place, I decided to go to mass at St. Basil's Church, which is on the St. Michael's campus. I was moved to tears during the gospel as I felt reassured that everything would go well. I also believed that God was confirming something about the insights I shared in the final chapter of my study.

In that chapter, I noted that we need to offer a more developed understanding of salvation to all people: not only Christians, but members of other religious traditions as well. In response to this challenge, I offered my own definition of salvation based on the fulfillment of the petitions of the Lord's Prayer.

This book expands on the insights found in the final chapter of my dissertation. In 2005, as I was working on that chapter, Fr. Gerard Bergie (now Auxiliary Bishop) was the pastor at my parish, St. Margaret Mary Parish in Hamilton. He and Susanne King, the chair of the parish council, asked me to facilitate a three-week lecture series on healing and salvation. In these lectures, I made the connection between being made well and the following actions: forgiveness, conversion, doing God's will, liberation, deliverance, and, finally, salvation. Susanne, who facilitated the prayer services for the first two sessions, asked me to choose a prayer for the third and final session. As I prayed for the right prayer to end our evening on healing and salvation, I thought of the Lord's Prayer. This prayer, I believed, captured my theology of salvation. It was this insight that led me to complete the final chapter of my dissertation.

The first draft of the final chapter was very long, as I was passionate about offering my own understanding of salvation. My thesis director, Dr. Margaret O'Gara, suggested that I include only a summary and create a new text based on the extensive commentary. *On Earth as it is in Heaven* is the result of three years of editing and reflection and 40 years of life experience. This book was born out of my search for the meaning of salvation, my work as a theologian, my personal and professional experience, and my involvement with parish ministry. It is part of a lifelong quest to bring the deeper meaning of salvation to all people.

Understanding the Gift of Salvation

Today there is a hunger for books that teach the Christian faith as a whole. People are looking for information that is integrated and holistic. Students of divinity, theology, and pastoral ministry are training to be our future pastoral ministers, educators, theologians, and clergy. As they will be ministering to whole persons, they need books and courses whose approach to theology and pastoral ministry are realistic and visionary. Without a doubt, the best resources and courses should be spiritual, intellectual, and practical.

This book has two major aims. First, it provides an "unofficial" fuller definition of salvation for Catholic Christians who are searching for the meaning of the Christian mystery of salvation. I will guide readers through the seven petitions of Matthew's version of the Lord's Prayer, examining their holistic, spiritual, psychological, social, physical, and otherworldly implications. Salvation, to be sure, is meant to be a universal experience, accessible to all people.

Second, the book offers pastors, theologians, lay ministers, and all Christians a definition of "integral salvation" for the whole person. The discussion blends insights from the social and natural sciences to show the body, mind, spirit implications of God's offer of salvation.

This is not meant to be an overly technical study of the Lord's Prayer; rather, I address the pastoral implications of salvation. At times, our understanding of salvation is overly simplified; at other times, we find it all too easy to leave it in the realm of mystery. People of faith need a deeper and more practical understanding of this great gift that God gives us through the grace of Jesus Christ.

I have found that many Christians are unsure about the deeper meaning of the gift of salvation. They know that salvation is accomplished in Jesus Christ, but may not be sure about what this means for them. I suggest that the fullness of the gospel and the meaning of salvation are found in the Lord's Prayer. The gift of salvation brings about transformation here and now as well as in the afterlife. A fuller definition of salvation, based on the Lord's Prayer, could help us preach the Good News. We are taught that Jesus died for us: for our sins and our salvation. This is true; this is the core of our faith as Christians. There is, however, something else Jesus does for us: what Jesus does *for* us is what he does *in* us. Following Jesus and his way should lead to change in our lives. We become new people with new understanding and insight into God's love and care for us. Jesus, the New Adam, shows us how to become the New Josephine, the New Robert, the New Anna, the New Gerard.

Salvation involves a way of life that is inspired by God's will and God's desire for our healing and deliverance. Some Christians have been taught to understand salvation as union with God. Mystics throughout the ages have affirmed that the desire for this union can be met in this lifetime. We are all called to be mystics—that is, people who seek union with God. Having union with God means we have been delivered from everything that drove us away from God.

Jesus delivered and healed the whole person, not just the body. His miracles of physical healing gave hope and peace to the mind and the soul. Health, as discussed in this book, involves more than physical wellness. A person may have a healthy body but a mind that does not perceive well, due to inner pain and loss. Christ came to restore all that has been lost. He gave physical sight to the physically blind, but he also gave spiritual sight to the spiritually blind. Some of us hear, but do not truly hear. Some of us see, but do not see the truth. At times, our pain and pride prevent us from seeing truth. Our hurts cause us to feel and see things that are not of God. Correcting our perception comes when our minds are healed. Jesus experienced non-stop union with God. St. Paul calls us to put on the mind of Christ so we can think like Christ. Once we have been healed of all distorted thinking, we can think and see clearly.

Salvation in the New Testament

In several places, the New Testament uses a Greek word for salvation that means "health," or "to be made well." The scriptures often express what God does in Jesus as "salvation." Many scholars agree that this term refers to bodily welfare or healing, deliverance, and a proper relationship with God, which implies a spiritual dimension. Also, the word "salvation" is derived from the Latin word *salus*, which means "health." The word "holy," too, comes from the Latin word for "health." The problem today is that we want to be "holy" without being "healed," without having wholeness of body, mind, and spirit. In several places in the New Testament, the gift of faith is linked with this concept of healing—being "made well" or saved.

The terms "being made well" or "saved" are often found in the words Jesus uses after a miracle of healing. In Mark's gospel, for example, we hear of the woman who has been suffering from hemorrhages for twelve years. She approaches Jesus, for she has faith that he can heal her. Moved by her faith, he says, "Daughter, your faith has made you well; go in peace and be healed of your disease" (5:34). This story inspires us to trust in our God, who desires to make us well, to save us. Humility and trust are part of the healing process.

This belief, then, begins the journey. My theology of salvation is rooted in the New Testament view that God desires to make us well both here and in the world to come. Jesus is the way to this spiritual, psychological, social, and physical health. He gives us a road map in the form of the Lord's Prayer. It is not enough to know that we are saved by Jesus Christ; he wants us to know what this means. The desire to be made well is universal; hence, the message of the Lord's Prayer is for all people, not just Christians.

Jesus' ministry was inclusive: he often taught, healed, and ate with those who were considered outsiders, outcasts, and unclean. If we are to follow Jesus, we cannot exclude anyone in our quest for healing and salvation.

Some verses from scripture associate salvation with healing or wellness; others associate this gift with being rescued from the dangers of this life. When Jesus encourages Peter to join him and walk on water, Peter begins to sink. He calls out, "Lord, save me!" (Matthew 14:30). In this case, salvation means deliverance from fear and danger. In Luke's gospel, Zechariah prophesies that his son, John the Baptist, will prepare the way for the Lord and "give knowledge of salvation to his people by the forgiveness of their sins" (Luke 1:77). Forgiveness of sins is connected to knowledge of salvation. Elsewhere in Luke we hear of the conversion of Zacchaeus, the tax collector; after the man's change of heart, Jesus says, "Today salvation has come to this house, because he too is a son of Abraham. For the Son of Man came to seek out and to save the lost" (Luke 19:9-10). Here Jesus is saying that conversion leads to salvation. As a tax collector, Zacchaeus was considered unworthy of welcome or hospitality. Jesus shows him that he is worthy of these things and calls him a "son of Abraham."

Luke's gospel features many powerful stories about being lost, then found and saved. For example, the story of the prodigal son in chapter 15 shows that God rewards sincere contrition, sorrow for one's sins, with mercy and a warm welcome. The merciful father does not shame the son by reminding him of past mistakes; instead, the father is thrilled that his son has turned his life around. This father is a model for all parents who have experienced pain and disappointment. When those we love return to us after a painful journey, we help their healing when we affirm and encourage them. We delay their healing when we remind them of their past mistakes, which shames them and communicates judgment and rejection rather than mercy. Mercy in turn communicates God's love, whether we feel someone deserves it or not. Salvation in these stories is connected to beginning a new life and turning away from harmful habits and thoughts. The Parable of the Judgment of Nations in the gospel of Matthew, however, reminds us of the connection between our earthly actions and everlasting life with God beyond the grave (Matthew 25:21-46). The process of salvation begins in this lifetime and is fulfilled in heaven.

In his letter to the Philippians, St. Paul calls on us to be lights in the world and to work out our own salvation (Philippians 2:12). While we receive salvation in Jesus Christ, salvation is a process. We need to cooperate with God's grace so we can become the people God has called us to be. The Lord's Prayer helps us to understand the various dimensions of this mystery.

As I said earlier, my theology of salvation is inspired by the Lord's Prayer: *Salvation is the fulfillment of the Lord's Prayer in individuals, communities, and in all of God's creation, in this lifetime and in the next.* Salvation, for me, is more than membership in a religious community, more than a single experience, thought, or belief. Rather, inspired by God's grace given through Jesus Christ, salvation is a succession of experiences, insights, actions, and beliefs that reconcile us to one another and to God in this life and in the life to come. In other words, salvation involves the process of sanctification. The Lord's Prayer presents the sincere will of God, our loving "Father," to save us. The Lord's Prayer "is truly the summary of the whole gospel" (*Catechism of the Catholic Church*, 2761, quoting Tertullian). The Good News of Jesus Christ is that he wants us to experience healing and transformation. He wants us to have the same intimate relationship with God "our Father." He wants us to experience true freedom and salvation. Salvation, in many ways, restores God's image in us. While we are created in the image and likeness of God, our struggles and weaknesses distort this image. By cooperating with God's will, God's image can be restored in us. This restoration, however, does not happen overnight.

What does occur in a moment is the beginning of faith, as it starts with a response to God. This response indicates trust and hope. For some people, the response is a sign of conversion. Salvation, then, begins with faith. Faith leads to changes in thought, word, and action. These changes restore our relationship with God (justification) and lead to sanctification. Sanctification literally means being made whole or well. It means being made holy. God's grace given to us through Jesus Christ, and our cooperation with God's will, bring about the sanctification that leads to salvation.

Through the Lord's Prayer, Jesus reveals the way to this restoration. God accepts our repentance; forgives our sins; calls us to forgive ourselves and others; heals our shame and guilt; liberates us from thoughts and habits that frustrate freedom; delivers us from oppression, addiction, and our fears; and leads us to everlasting life. What is more, the mystery of salvation is multi-dimensional. It is worldly and otherworldly, personal and communal. It expresses God's great love for creation. Understanding salvation as the fulfillment of the Lord's Prayer, in this world and in the next, addresses the physical, spiritual, and universal needs of individuals and communities. Too often, people limit salvation to the afterlife: going to heaven. While salvation does include eternal life with God, it can begin in the present. If it begins in the present, it must involve change in our everyday lives. Recall that the Lord's Prayer calls for our actions on earth to be as those in heaven: "thy will be done on earth as it is in heaven." Salvation is a gift that is concerned with conversion, liberation, deliverance, and healing. Understood in this way, salvation relates to men and women of all races, classes, cultures, and religions.

The Lord's Prayer is a prayer of "integral salvation, one which embraces the whole person and all mankind ..." (*Redemptoris Missio,* 11). Jesus is a "sneak preview" of what God wills for all people—a sneak preview of who God is and a sneak preview of our own calling. Jesus reveals to us our healed and integrated selves. His message and ministry are relevant to all people, as the desire for wholeness and reconciliation with God and with each other is universal. Any understanding of salvation needs to consider the whole person, whole communities, and all of God's creation, the environment and all of God's creatures, in the present and in the world to come.

God wants all people to know salvation. God our Saviour "desires everyone to be saved and to come to the knowledge of the truth. For there is one God; there is also one mediator between God and humankind, Christ Jesus himself human" (1 Timothy 2:4-5). Jesus' mediation involves saving us. In Luke's gospel we hear about the Annunciation, when the angel Gabriel appears to Mary and tells her that she will give birth to the Son of the Most High. She is to name him "Jesus." Jesus is the Greek version of the Hebrew *Yeshua*, or Joshua. His name literally means "God saves." In Matthew's gospel, the angel of the Lord tells Joseph not to be afraid to take Mary as his wife, as her son is from the Holy Spirit and he will "save his people from their sins." In Jesus, God saves and calls us out of the darkness and delivers us from the various forms of slavery that exist. We can be enslaved to destructive habits. We can be enslaved to debt. We can be enslaved to negative thinking and pride. We can be enslaved to all kinds of sin.

The Second Vatican Council (1962–65), a gathering of all the bishops of the Catholic Church, affirmed the salvation of the whole person: body, mind, and spirit. If salvation involves the body, then salvation begins today. We are not to put it off, so that the process of restoration begins only at death. The bishops at the Second Vatican Council taught that God wills the world to experience salvation with Christ. The Council declared that salvation includes the world's union with God and unity with one another. This unity is true communion. The salvation that Christ brings restores and renews. Jesus restores in us our likeness to God.

In the beginning, we were created fully restored. Poor choices and habits distort this image. Think of people you know who are compassionate, kind, loving, faithful, and generous. Chances are that you like to be with them. Their presence is inviting and warm. You feel welcome. On the other hand, think of people who are abusive, full of resentment, angry, and rude. You probably feel uncomfortable and fearful in their presence. God wants to restore God's image in us so that we can be saved. The process of being saved will lead to the increase of feeling God's presence in everyone, so that all are healed of their hurts.

Like a seed, God is in each one of us. Some people nourish the seed with love and humility. Others prevent it from growing through pride and resentment. Jesus is the way to growth and restoration. This restoration and renewal is not limited to Christians alone; God desires to extend this good news to all people, no matter what their religious beliefs (*Gaudium et Spes*, 22.) Before Christians can speak of salvation to members of other religions, however, we need to understand what we want others to experience. We cannot offer a gift and not know what it is ourselves.

We are called to communicate this gift to all people, in the present. If we have experienced the transformation that comes with being saved, others will look at us and want to experience the same thing. Think of the people you know who are positive and full of joy. What makes them that way? What are they doing that is different? Could a person who is constantly negative and resentful teach you how to be joyful? The gift of salvation must be lived. Unlike other gifts, it is a transforming experience with visible effects. People need to see it. Think of Simeon in Luke's gospel. Simeon is described as a righteous and devout man. "It had been revealed to him by the Holy Spirit that he would not see death before he had seen the Lord's Messiah" (Luke 2:26). When Mary and Joseph bring the infant Jesus to the temple, Simeon takes the baby into his arms and says, "Master, now you are dismissing your servant in peace, according to your word; for my eyes have seen your salvation, which you have prepared in the presence of all peoples, a light for revelation to the Gentiles and for glory to your people Israel."

Simeon saw salvation in Jesus Christ. If we become like Jesus, others will see salvation in us. To appreciate this gift, we must see it and know what it is. To see Jesus is to see salvation. To see someone restored and healed is to see salvation. Simeon reminds us that Jesus was not to be limited to the people of Israel; he was also to be "a light for revelation to the Gentiles"—in other words, non-Jews.

The message of salvation is therefore for all people. It is inclusive. That is why we need to communicate the message of salvation by living it. Like Simeon, we can hope to see salvation before we die. The Lord's Prayer shows us how we can be transformed so that others can see salvation in us, here and now. Let us begin our journey into the most important prayer in Christian history.

Introduction
to the Lord's Prayer

S t. Augustine wrote, "Run through all the words of the holy prayers [in Scripture], and I do not think that you will find anything in them that is not contained and included in the Lord's Prayer."[1] St. Thomas Aquinas spoke of his own reverence for this prayer:

> The Lord's Prayer is the most perfect of prayers .... In it we ask, not only for all the things we can rightly desire, but also in the sequence that they should be desired. This prayer not only teaches us to ask for things, but also in what order we should desire them.[2]

A contemporary theologian, Leonardo Boff, follows suit in his study of the Lord's Prayer:

> In the Lord's Prayer we encounter in a practical way the correct relationship between God and humankind, between heaven and earth, between the religious and the political, while maintaining unity throughout. The first part speaks on God's behalf: the Father, keeping his

name holy, his kingdom, his holy will. The second part is concerned with human interests: our daily bread, for-giveness, ever-present temptation, and ever-threatening evil.[3]

The Lord's Prayer, then, is a prayer with deep insight into human need and the need for reconciliation and unity with God. "The *order* in which the petitions appear is not arbitrary."[4] They begin with God as our starting point, then, move to our needs as they relate to the kingdom. Our plight on earth is connected to our hope in heaven.

While "the historical formula given by Jesus himself is not accessible to us,"[5] some scholars note that two ver-sions of the Lord's Prayer, as found in Luke (11:2-4) and Matthew (6:9-13), were compiled somewhere between 75 and 85 A.D.[6] The shorter version, found in Luke, is believed to be closer to the original,[7] and is intended to show Gen-tiles (non-Jews) how to pray. The longer version, found in Matthew, is "slanted to Jews who know how to pray and need only learn how to pray correctly …."[8] I have chosen to use the longer version, from the gospel of Matthew, as it is closest to the one that people use most often in public and private prayer and because its petitions best capture my understanding of integral salvation.

Here is Matthew's version of the Lord's Prayer:

Our Father in heaven, hallowed be your name.
Your kingdom come.
Your will be done, on earth as it is in heaven.
Give us this day our daily bread.
And forgive us our debts, as we also have forgiven
   our debtors.
And do not bring us to the time of trial, but
   rescue us from the evil one.

The Lord's Prayer has its roots in Judaism. It is similar to the Shemoneh Esre, a Jewish prayer with eighteen blessings[9] that was recited by Jews in Jesus' time. This prayer is divided into three general types: praise, petitions, and thanksgiving. The prayers of praise affirm the holiness of God's name; the petitions focus on repentance, forgiveness, redemption, restoration of justice, knowledge, and healing. The final blessings express thanks for peace.

The first Christian communities began to pray the Lord's Prayer three times a day in place of the eighteen blessings.[10] In time, the prayer was included in the liturgical life of early Christians, and has remained in the Church's liturgical prayer ever since.

Our Father in heaven

The first two words of this prayer reveal God's desire to be close to us. Jesus includes us in his intimacy with his "Father." With Jesus, we share a common bond. He is our elder brother on the journey and is calling on God to take us on as God's children. God is concerned for all of us; Jesus shows us how to call out to God. Note that Jesus does not say, "*My* Father in heaven." The plural "our" reveals our common foundation and home in God. Jesus' "Father" is the "Father" of all people. We are brothers and sisters in our pursuit of fulfillment. If God is a parent to all people, this implies something unique about our relationship with one another, despite differences in gender, culture, race, ethnicity, age, religious affiliation, and social class. We are brothers and sisters in Jesus Christ. God's desire for intimacy is not partial to any one person or group. God's desire for intimacy with us is universal.

Perhaps the most uplifting feature of this prayer is found in the way Jesus refers to God as "Father" or, more accurately, "Daddy." The author of Matthew's gospel preserves the Aramaic term *Abba*, which means "Daddy" or "Dad" or "dearest father." It is a term of endearment meant to show intimacy and respect. Unlike others during his day, Jesus chose to use this word when praying to God. In fact, he uses it 170 times in the gospels. Biblical scholars tell us that it was very unusual to use a familiar term to refer to God. Clearly, Jesus wants us to consider how close God is to us. When we were children, our parents were probably the people closest to us. What better way to show God's closeness than to describe God as a loving father? Jesus pushes this insight even further by calling God the familial "Daddy" rather than the more formal "Father."

How many of us today call our parents "Mother" or "Father"? In Italian, father is *padre* and mother is *madre*. As a child, I called my parents *Papa* and *Mamma* (Daddy and Mommy in Italian). In my adult years, I called them Ma and Pa. It would have felt so formal and strange to call them "Mother" (*madre*) and "Father" (*padre*). Leonardo Boff notes that "Daddy" belongs to the language of childhood. Remember that Jesus called us to be like children. Like a child runs to her "daddy," we, too, run to our God.

Some people have false images of God. They may perceive God as full of wrath and judgment, waiting to punish and condemn. Calling God "Daddy" heals our understanding of God and encourages us to develop positive images of God: God as loving and merciful, kind and approachable. "Daddy" is inviting; this word soothes our fears.

"Daddy" suggests that "Our Father in heaven" is a God who is intimate with God's children, like a "daddy." God is our "daddy" every second of every day. Greg Anderson, a man who experienced great healing, was comforted through his meditation on the Lord's Prayer. In his writing on cancer and the Lord's Prayer, he encourages us "to stop saying 'Our Father' on Sunday, only to spend the rest of the week living like an orphan."[11] If we pray the Lord's Prayer with openness and sincerity, we will take the prayer seriously and will accept God's offer to parent us in an intimate way. God wants to walk with us each day and guide us like a loving parent.

God is there to pick up the pieces whenever human parents fail to provide the intimacy that both children and adult children need. Research in the area of childhood development provides proof that children need love and human affection in their formative years if they are to grow up to be healthy adults. I remember watching a documentary on PBS that had filmed a number of psychologists following and studying a group of orphans in Eastern Europe. Throughout the study, the psychologists documented the orphans' psychological responses and growth. The researchers found that those who experienced a lack of love and human affection from birth grew up to be developmentally delayed. They did not experience normal psychological development due to extreme neglect. This neglect prevented their brains from releasing a growth hormone. Also, their consciences did not form. Children need attentive and loving parents. Adults, too, need attentive and loving guidance. If we are open to growing spiritually, we must be open to being parented by God.

Fifteen years ago, a dear friend of mine lost her father. Her mother had died many years before. At the time, I was in my mid-20s. My father had died when I was 23, but my mother was still alive and quite healthy. While I could relate to my friend's loss, I could not comprehend all of her pain. This time her grief had a new dimension; she felt like an orphan. She felt alone and was parentless. She was married with four children, but they could not fill the void. She missed being someone's daughter. She felt as though she had lost her connection to her roots, to her home base.

When my mother died eight years ago, I thought of my friend. I finally knew what she was feeling. No matter how old we are, we need to feel connected and loved. Like my friend, I am married with four children, but, at times, I still want someone to care for me like a parent. For eight years, I was a single parent of two beautiful children, Teresa and Eriberto. My mother was my surrogate spouse, as she provided for us in many ways. We had a deal. I would go over to her house and make dinner for us each night, and she would wash the dishes afterwards. If you knew me well, you would know that I was very happy with this arrangement! On days that I was sick or feeling exhausted, she would encourage me to come over so that she could make tea and toast for me. These seem like small things, but it was nice to have someone take care of me. As she got older, I tried to return the favour. I helped her take care of her home and her own health care needs. She passed away after I remarried, but was blessed to see the birth of my third child, my son Aniello. Even now I miss her. I still crave the affection of a mother, someone to nurture me. I'm sure many people feel this way. The good news is that God is the ultimate parent—more than a surrogate, and more than a human parent.

God's love and concern are rooted in the intimacy that Jesus implies in the Lord's Prayer. In his commentary on this verse, Boff asks an important question: "How shall we pray the Lord's Prayer in a Fatherless World?"[12] Leonardo Boff, who is from Brazil, has written about the struggle many women face when they are abandoned by their husbands. He has observed first-hand the great challenge of raising children in underprivileged communities. In many cases, grandparents step in to help their daughters raise the children. In other areas, fathers take on new roles. Men and women all over the world are reassessing their roles as mothers and fathers. While it is beyond the scope of this work to examine the social implications of the use of "Father" in the Lord's Prayer, it is worthwhile noting that Jesus' reference to God as "Father" implies a positive, life-giving relationship with the God who desires to be worshipped and understood as a loving and merciful parent: an anchor, foundation, trusted guide, and lover of humanity.

According to a recent study, since 1980, the percentage of children who live with two married parents has gone down 9%.[13] In 2004, nearly one-quarter (23%) of children lived only with their mothers. This means that many children are living in a temporarily or permanently fatherless world. While most single mothers are able to manage the demands of responsible parenting, the assistance and support offered by a child's father can alleviate some of the stress that comes with parenting in the 21st century. Although mothers need emotional and psychological support from the fathers of their children, the lack of financial support, especially in the case of single parenting, can be devastating. Meanwhile, many fathers would like more access to their children. In some cases, the courts have decided how "fatherless" or "motherless" some families are. Many parents may not desire their current situation; they may want to be with their children every day. This is the pain of divorce—a change in the way and how often we see our children. My older children expressed this grief often. They grieved having lost access to both parents at the same time.

The challenge of raising children alone, without emotional and spiritual support, can make matters worse. Here in Canada, a Statistics Canada study completed in 1994–95 surveyed 23,000 children during an eight-month period.[14] The study found that children raised by single mothers face increased risks of emotional, behavioural, academic, and social problems. This finding does not suggest that single mothers are worse parents; rather, the challenge of juggling parental, social, economic, and personal responsibilities makes it more difficult to meet children's needs. Single fathers face the same dilemmas. If we add a painful divorce, death, illness, abandonment or poverty to the situation, the stress levels increase substantially. Even the most stable and secure homes experience ongoing stress when raising children. Two married parents who have a loving bond also face many trials in raising a family. For single parents, it can be an overwhelming situation.

Imagine someone who is grieving the breakdown of a marriage. Imagine someone whose spouse has died. Imagine someone trying to cope with the everyday needs of children while being consumed with grief and pain. Imagine that this person must also find new housing, pay the bills, manage a new schedule, and provide a safe and secure environment for his or her children. While friends and family may extend helping hands and a shoulder to lean on, only someone who has gone through the same experience can know the pain and chaos that accompany this kind of loss. At times, God alone can offer comfort and release. God fills the void with hope and courage to get the person through one day at a time.

Imagine someone who has been diagnosed with a serious illness. Imagine a couple who buys a new home just before one spouse loses his or her job—the job that was going to carry most of the bills. Single people, too, need to draw on God's love and support as they face the challenges of each day. A theologian once said that loneliness is the biggest challenge we face today. People, whether they are married or single, need intimacy. Sometimes the "intimacy" that the world offers is shallow. It leaves us wanting more. Suffering due to loneliness is universal.

When one person suffers, the whole family feels it. There is no rest. When both spouses are suffering, it may be difficult to reach out to each other. Individual spouses need comfort and understanding. A spouse who is in pain of some kind may not have the strength to carry the other. God helps couples in their pain and provides the support that may not come from our loved ones. I have learned that I cannot survive challenges on my own. While my husband is a wonderful source of support, it would be unfair to place all of my hope for support on his shoulders. Like me, he struggles sometimes. He needs reassurance and a steady show of comfort. God alone can provide this consistent support on the days that are too hard to bear. Like Jesus, we can call on God's assistance and strength. We were not meant to carry burdens alone.

I have seen people go through terrible tragedies. As a former campus minister and parish minister, I noticed a difference in those families who have a deep faith. They have an unusual resilience. They could get through tough times. Those who do not seek God's offer of help can manage, but it may be more difficult for them.

Families of all shapes and sizes experience change and struggle. If we love, we will have new demands. Parenting can be a life-changing experience. The Lord's Prayer shows us that God is a model for all parents. If we invite God into our families, God is sure to surprise us with God's providence.

Jesus' use of the name *Abba* teaches us something about who God is and about the unique relationship God wants to have with us. This relationship is not to be distant, impersonal, and limited. Instead, it is a relationship that is rooted in intimacy, trust, and connectedness. It can offer hope and restoration, especially in places where unconditional love and support are lacking. Parents who are open to Jesus' insights can learn from him that being a parent involves physical and emotional presence, loyalty, unconditional love, and support. Jesus' endearing way of communicating with his God reveals to us the ideal relationship between a parent and a child. Any parent-child relationship that lacks emotional, physical, or spiritual support reveals a distorted understanding of the parent-child relationship that God desires. God's presence in our lives is limitless. It is not bound by our inadequacies, fears, and misunderstandings.

God is in Heaven

The Lord's Prayer reminds us of this point as we praise our God who is *in heaven*. As the saying goes, "Live as though heaven is on earth." Something special is expressed here. Peace, joy, love, and happiness are not things we will experience only in the afterlife. Our connectedness to God implies that God wants us to experience great things now. That God is said to be in heaven tells us something else about God's being. Jesus is saying that God is not limited to our earthly understanding of the world. Our relationship with God reaches far beyond the boundaries of our earthly existence. While we can experience a taste of heaven here on earth, this part of the Lord's Prayer reminds us that heaven is a home for us: "(h)eaven, not earth, is our homeland."[15] I would argue, however, that we may experience moments of heaven on earth, whenever we do God's will and are surrounded by others who do the same. While the ideal is perfect peace, I have learned to cherish perfect moments—moments when I know that I am exactly where God wants me to be. We all know this feeling, which comes when we are around people who communicate Christ's love and charisma. We want be around these people, who offer light and encouragement. The irresistible Christ is working through them.

Perfect peace comes with decades of spiritual work. With God's grace, peace will come from within, but first we must have a disciplined prayer life and trust in God. We will know we have attained this state of inner peace when we can deal with all the trials and sorrows in our lives and still manage to maintain our inner peace. A wise person once told me, "Josie, you must imagine yourself on a tightrope and picture Jesus and the truth at the end of the tightrope. As you are walking toward Jesus, people begin to shout. On one side people shout: 'Great work! You are the best!' Be careful, however, as pride and ego may cause you to look down and you will fall. On the other side, people shout: 'You are terrible. You cannot do this. You are going to fall!' If you let them get to you, you may look down at them and you will fall. You must maintain your peace at all cost. Jesus and the truth are your focus." In order to maintain my peace throughout the years, I have worked on the following goals: not to let affirmation go to my head, nor criticism get to my heart. I call this state "holy indifference."

Whenever we are attached to the views of others, we are enslaved. While affirmation is positive, it can lead to inflated egos. Instead, we are called to be thankful and bless God for the gift. We are instruments; we should be thankful if our work is bearing fruit, but watch for pride and ego. It is easier to view others as equals if we see our gifts as coming from God. Mean-spirited criticism, on the other hand, tears us down. Sincere, spirit-filled correction is helpful and should be delivered with kindness. Received with humility, correction can lead to great things. Attachment to either praise or criticism can rob us of our peace. Accept compliments and bless God; receive correction in the right spirit and ask for God's blessing; correct the mistake and let it go.

There are many spiritual insights that God wants us to experience here and now. However, we need peace so we can handle the surprises of each day. While this earth can never capture the glory of heaven, God wants to give us some of the spiritual riches of heaven so we can grow and prepare for the greater glory. The scriptures remind us of those heavenly insights that can be gained on earth:

> Surely, this commandment that I am commanding you today is not too hard for you, nor is it too far away. It is not in heaven, that you should say, "Who will go up to heaven for us, and get it for us so that we may hear it and observe it?" Neither is it beyond the sea, that you should

say, "Who will cross to the other side of the sea for us, and get it for us so that we may hear it and observe it?" No, the word is very near to you, it is in your mouth and in your heart for you to observe. (Deuteronomy 30:11-14)

This passage teaches us that God's will for us is not hard to find. It is not in some far-off place. Nor should we be passive and wait for someone to get it for us. It is very near to us; it is in our mouths and in our hearts. Jesus teaches us that God in heaven desires that we experience the joys of this heaven. Our God who is in heaven loves us so much that God wants us, as is taught in the petitions that follow this opening line of the Lord's Prayer, to share in God's majesty and wonder. Also, we are reminded of the need to honour and praise God, who is constantly calling us to the intimacy that exists between parent and child. God wants to give us a foretaste of heaven. God prepares our hearts with peace so we can receive these gifts.

Reflection questions

- What is your understanding of God?
- Are your images of God positive or negative? In what way? How can you start to revise any negative ones?
- Can you relate to the concept of God as "Father"/ parent? How? If not, how can you begin to see God in this way?
- Have you invited God's "fatherly care" into your home and family? If yes, how? If no, how could you do this?

Prayer

Loving God, we thank you for calling us your children.

We thank you for Jesus our Saviour and elder brother.

Grant that we may learn to parent and love each other with the love Jesus shared with you.

May wisdom, patience, and endurance be with all those who seek your will and guidance.

Amen.

Hallowed be your name

Petition #1: *Hallowed be your name*

We begin the Lord's Prayer by recognizing God our "Father," whose presence is boundless and universal. This first petition calls us toward God. The verb "to hallow" speaks of adoration, praise, and thanksgiving; in other words, we are to acknowledge the holiness of God's name. As the first blessings of the Jewish prayer the Eighteen Blessings do, we affirm and praise God. The holiness of God's name is spoken of throughout the scriptures. According to a vision of the prophet Isaiah, seraphs, who were in attendance above the Lord, called to one another and said: "Holy, holy, holy is the Lord of hosts; the whole earth is full of his glory" (Isaiah 6:3). In Luke's gospel, angels rejoice at the birth of Jesus, saying, "Glory to God in the highest heaven, and on earth peace among those whom he favours" (Luke 2:14). We honour God's name when we worship and pray, but we are called to honour his name through our actions, thoughts, and words as well.

God calls God's people to holiness, as God is holy (Ezek. 20:9). Jesus, in Matthew's gospel, reminds us to "[b]e perfect, therefore, as your heavenly Father is perfect" (5:48). In this context, "perfect" means "made whole." Jesus is calling us to be whole, to be made well, to be restored. While this petition suggests that God's being is something other than our being, we are challenged to honour and respect God and be like God. St. Peter Chrysologus, one of the early fathers of the Church, makes the connection between the holiness of God's name and God's desire to offer salvation to us:

> We ask God to hallow his name, which by its own holiness saves and makes holy all creation …. It is this name that gives salvation to a lost world. But we ask that this name of God should be hallowed in us through our actions. For God's name is blessed when we live well, but is blasphemed when we live wickedly. As the Apostle says: "The name of God is blasphemed among the Gentiles because of you." We ask then that, just as the name of God is holy, so we may obtain his holiness in our souls.[16]

God's own holiness desires to be united with our holiness. True union with God happens when we give back to God the image God gave us—in its original state. This implies a certain level of responsibility on our part. For Christians, responsibility means carrying out our promises to follow the commandments, living our baptismal promises, and loving self, others, and God. This means we are called to sanctification. As we become more and more

self-aware—of our thoughts, words, deeds, and choices—
we should be moving closer and closer to thoughts, words,
deeds, choices, and relationships that are fulfilling and life-
giving. This inner transformation will lead to our sanctification, and our lives will give God the glory that is desired.
A lack of social, individual, and communal responsibility,
on the other hand, dishonours God and us.

This first petition acknowledges the universal call to
holiness, a topic that was heavily emphasized in the teaching of the bishops at the Second Vatican Council:

> It is quite clear that all Christians in any state or walk of
> life are called to the fullness of Christian life and to the
> perfection of love, and by this the perfection of love, and
> by this holiness a more human manner of life is fostered
> also in earthly society. In order to reach this perfection
> the faithful should use the strength dealt out to them
> by Christ's gift, so that, following in his footsteps and
> conformed in his image, doing the will of God in eve-
> rything, they may wholeheartedly devote themselves to
> the glory of God and to the service of their neighbour.
> Thus the holiness of the People of God will grow in
> fruitful abundance, as is clearly shown in the history of
> the Church through the life of so many saints. (*Lumen
> Gentium*, 39)

The official teaching of the Catholic Church calls all
people, regardless of their state of life, to holiness. Many
Christians may believe that clergy are more favoured by
God. Or they may believe that God calls a select few to

be holy. This is not true. State of life does not guarantee sanctification. Our will to be made holy, coupled with God's grace, bring sanctification. Our states of life can be used as instruments of this sanctification. Our service to others, our relationships, our joys and our sorrows, our prayer life, and our life experiences lead us toward wholeness in God. God wants all people to be holy. We are all called to serve one another in a variety of vocations and ministries. All people contribute to society, and God is pleased whenever and wherever we are fulfilling God's plan for us. A parent lives out his or her salvation in caring for the family. A medical doctor lives out her salvation as she provides health care for her patients. A farmer or auto technician is living out his salvation as he works the field or services someone's vehicle.

Admitting the need to be made holy or sanctified is a natural first step toward salvation. This step can take place in a range of settings, as long as the setting is a life-giving one. If the setting or our work leads to destruction or pain, we are called to seek out a path that is fulfilling so that God's plan can be realized. We cannot bear fruit when our work goes against God's will. If a person is hired to lie and cheat, or to exploit workers, the fruits of these actions are anxiety, worry, and oppression. God does not will that we feel anxious or worried. On the other hand, if a person is hired to contribute to society in a sincere and meaningful way, the person will feel some satisfaction and peace. Faith and trust in God are the first step: they lead us to work that is life-giving. Changing careers requires deep

faith and trust in God. The second step involves justification, or being made righteous. Our relationship with God
is restored as we are made right with God. When we find
meaningful work that is pleasing to God, we honour God.
The Holy Spirit assists with this transformation. The Spirit
sanctifies us and prepares us for the kingdom. Praising
God's name, then, requires us to change our actions. They
must give glory to God.

Blessing God requires disciplined speech as well. We
cannot honour God if we blaspheme, swear, or curse. We
cannot honour God if our speech is reckless, abusive, and
irresponsible. Countless proverbs and other scriptural
teachings warn against harmful speech. Jesus says, "I tell
you, on the day of judgment you will have to give an account
for every careless word you utter; for by your words you
will be justified, and by your words you will be condemned"
(Matthew 12:36). We cannot ask for God's help in one
breath and curse God and our brothers and sisters in the
next. Cursing cancels any blessing we ask for and does not
allow God's blessings to enter our lives. Discipline of speech
is one of the more difficult disciplines. Some people may not
put much thought into the implications of reckless speech,
only to discover the nightmares that follow irresponsible
words. We are called, therefore, to honour God with our
minds, hearts, actions, and words. Only holy words and
actions can give God glory.

Reflection questions

- How do you show honour to God's name?
- How do you live out your call to holiness? In your family? In the workplace? As a volunteer?

Prayer

*Creator God, we praise your holy name
and rejoice in your great love for us.*

*Grant that our words, thoughts, and actions
are disciplined*

*so that we may glorify your holy name
with our entire being.*

We ask this through Christ our Lord.

Amen.

Your kingdom come

Petition #2: *Your kingdom come*

What is God's kingdom or reign like? This second petition speaks of the arrival of God's reign on earth, where love, justice, hope, and balance will be restored. In his letter to Titus, Paul writes:

> For the grace of God has appeared, bringing salvation to all, training us to renounce impiety and worldly passions, and in the present age to live lives that are self-controlled, upright and godly, while we wait for the blessed hope and the manifestation of the glory of our great God and saviour, Jesus Christ. He it is who gave himself for us that he might redeem us from all iniquity and purify for himself a people of his own who are zealous for good deeds. (2:11-14)

This means that God's reign will bring about purification. It is our responsibility, however, to work toward the coming of God's reign with right action and right thought.

In the above passage, St. Paul reminds us that we need to prepare for the glory of "our great God." This preparation involves changing those parts of our lives that are not disciplined. To be sure, this can be difficult. The demands of our culture can be overwhelming. We need the courage to invite God into our lives. The daughter of Martin Luther King was once interviewed regarding the trials of the present day. She said that we cannot shut God out of our public lives and ask God to intervene in only part of our lives. God's kingdom will come when God's ways are welcome in the workplace, in the family, and in all areas of our community.

One of my theology professors, Ovey Mohammed SJ, once said in class that for God's kingdom to come, ours must go: "Your kingdom come, my kingdom go!" This view suggests self-awareness and ongoing conversion and transformation of self and communities. "Kingdom does not refer here to a territory but to the divine power and authority that now is in this world, transforming the old into new, the unjust into just, and sickness into health."[17] Furthermore, as Jesus suggested, the kingdom is a process:

> The kingdom of heaven is like a mustard seed that someone took and sowed in his field; it is the smallest of all the seeds, but when it has grown it is the greatest of shrubs and becomes a tree, so that the birds of the air come and make nests in its branches .... The kingdom of heaven is like yeast that a woman took and mixed in with three measures of flour until all of it was leavened. (Matthew 13:31-33)

The seeds of the kingdom are found in individuals and communities. The more responsible we become, the more loving and compassionate our relationships, the more justice that is present in families and communities, the more integrated we become, the more righteous and Christ-like we become, the more God's kingdom will be present here on earth. The process will change us cell by cell, so that just as a seed becomes a tree, we will reflect God's image more and more here on earth. This transformation of individuals will transform communities into more just and egalitarian communities. Thich Nhat Hanh, a Buddhist monk, offers his own commentary on the parable of the mustard seed:

> Matthew described the Kingdom of God as being like a tiny mustard seed. It means that the seed of the Kingdom is God within us. If we know how to plant that seed in the moist soil of our daily lives, it will grow and become a large bush on which many birds can take refuge.[18]

This tree or large bush will, no doubt, go through trials and challenges. Our pursuit of the kingdom will involve different phases: seasons of drought and seasons of plenty. Seasons of drought may bring times of struggle related to loss, grief, pain, and sorrow. Seasons of plenty may bring times of joy, hope, restoration, and peace. While we grow in both of these seasons, we are called to be hopeful in seasons of drought and thankful in seasons of plenty. God's grace will not leave us abandoned and will help to bring about God's kingdom. Eventually, once the kingdom is fully alive in us, we shall become like Jesus—the evergreen tree. He is in full bloom in every season. The more we nurture the seed with hope, prayer, faith, love, charity, and understanding, it, like the yeast, will cause God's kingdom to grow within us and in our communities. We must desire the kingdom within ourselves before we see it alive in our surroundings: "So if anyone is in Christ, there is a new creation: everything old has passed away; see, everything has become new" (2 Cor. 5:17).

One of the classes I teach at St. Augustine's Seminary is Theological Anthropology. In this course, we discuss what it means to be human from a Christian perspective. We talk about Jesus as "The New Adam." St. Paul uses this language when he writes about the great gifts Jesus brings. Through him, God brings hope and salvation. Jesus, God incarnate, is the restored man. The good news is that we are all called to be made new. I tell my students that while I am not the "New Josephine," I am *becoming* the "New Josephine." Once we are transformed into the image God desires for us, God's kingdom is restored. We will talk, think, and act in ways that build community and restore God's creation.

Reflection questions

- What is your understanding of God's kingdom? Is it something we can experience in the present?

- Have you invited God's kingdom into your family, your workplace, your community?

- What needs to happen for your community to be transformed into God's kingdom?

Prayer

Merciful God, you know our struggles.

You know those things that keep us from being fulfilled in you.

Help us grow in love and understanding.

Grant that we may be open to the transformation you will for us.

Amen.

Your will be done, on earth as it is in heaven

Petition #3: *Your will be done, on earth as it is in heaven*

A person once asked a pastor, "How do we know what God's will is?" The pastor replied that we know God's will through the teachings of the scriptures. The Ten Commandments, for example, give us some direction on how to conduct ourselves in our families and our community. If a married person who is tempted to have an affair wonders what God's will is for this situation, consulting the commandments reveals the answer: adultery goes against God's will. If someone is tempted to steal, the scriptures offer some advice. We have been given some guidelines, through the scriptures, as to how to treat ourselves and each other. Apart from scripture, we have our ability to reason: our gut instinct tells us if something is wrong. Our consciences disturb us. This is what we call the "Natural Law." Our ability to reason informs our understanding. Reason and faith, then, work together to show us the logic behind God's will. At times, however, we may not trust God's will for us. We may feel that we know better.

From time to time, my students ask me to give them a definition of *original sin*. Over the years I have developed my own definition based on my life experiences: original sin is the illusion that we can find fulfillment outside of God's will. The garden is the place where God's will is fulfilled and we live in harmony with God. We trust God and his plan for us. Our ancestors did not trust his plan and ventured off on their own, believing that their will was superior, only to find out that they were enslaved by their distorted understanding of fulfillment. Following God's will justifies us and leads us back to the garden. God knows what is best for us and we are called to cooperate with his plan. Other scriptures affirm the proper quest for fulfillment.

The beatitudes teach us that those who thirst for righteousness and peace will be blessed (Matthew 5:1-11). Also, Jesus reminds us to love God with heart, mind, and soul and to love our neighbours as ourselves (Matthew 22:36-39). Finally, eternal life is for those who give food to the hungry, give drink to the thirsty, welcome strangers, and provide shelter and clothing for the naked (Matthew 25:31-46). Ultimately, love of self, others, and God is part of God's will. "Not everyone who says to me, 'Lord, Lord,' will enter the kingdom of heaven, but only the one who does the will of my Father in heaven," Jesus says (Matthew 7:21). Jesus calls people to be merciful (Matthew 12:7); those who do God's will are his "mothers, brothers, and sisters" (Matthew 12:50). The bishops of the Second Vatican Council called all Catholics to "persevere in charity," as this is what it means to respond to the grace of Christ and do God's will. We are called to respond in "thought, word, and deed" to show that we have been blessed with the grace of Christ (*Lumen Gentium*, 14).

Finally, God's will includes the salvation of all people, for God "desires everyone to be saved and to come to the knowledge of the truth" (1 Timothy 2:4). This salvation is willed for all people, whatever their gender, race, class, ethnicity, or religious affiliation. Through this prayer, Jesus shows us how to be saved. This process calls for transformation and sanctification. The social, personal, political, physical, and spiritual implications of the Lord's Prayer are universal. This gift of salvation implies God wills one experience for all people; this experience involves conversion, forgiveness, healing, growth, and deliverance. Aligning our wills with God's will helps to bring about this process. Our response to God's call to salvation is the first sign that we want to do God's will. We desire health and healing, deliverance, liberation from trial, forgiveness, basic human resources for survival, and the fruits of the kingdom: love, justice, and peace. In an earlier section of this book, I noted that heaven on earth, for me, is doing God's will perfectly and being surrounded by those who are in communion with God and God's will. While we continue to be challenged by the pain of illness and natural disasters, doing God's will and being in a community with others who do the same is calming and peaceful. It brings freedom and creates an environment built on trust and charity. Following God's will requires radical trust.

I have found that doing God's will brings true freedom. If one lies, cheats, steals, injures other people or hurts oneself, is this person free? The world may seduce us into thinking that doing whatever feels good is freedom. Instead, I have found that this kind of "freedom" enslaves. Think of a young person who is sexually active outside of marriage. When I was working as a high school chaplain, it was not unusual for a teenage girl to come to my office because she was afraid and anxious about a missed period. Is this freedom? What about a young guy who steals from work, only to be charged a month before he starts university. Does the anxiety of facing criminal charges bring freedom? Someone who gossips is afraid of being found out or being attacked for spreading rumours. Someone who lies lives in fear of being caught. There is no peace in maintaining a lie. These kinds of actions enslave us and create fear and trouble for ourselves and others. The truth, however, brings freedom. Following God's will, while it may appear demanding, is the only way to true freedom. There is peace and security to be found in obeying God's laws.

Think of a time when you were insulted or treated unfairly. Did you remain silent? If you stayed silent, you are not free. The bad behaviour remains uncorrected and you are held hostage by resentment and anger. Did you confront the person truthfully and tactfully? Then you are free. The truth does set us free. This is God's will. There is logic in God's plan. Think of adultery; it hurts people and families. It brings pain, despair, and feelings of betrayal. God desires what is best for us. God wants to direct our path so that we can be free from fear, resentment, and anxiety. "Is there anyone among you who, if your child asks for bread will give a stone? Or if the child asks for a fish, will give it a snake?" (Matthew 7:9-10). God, like human parents, wills for us those things that bring us fulfillment and freedom. Doing what we think feels right in the moment can lead to temporary and shallow pleasure.

Doing God's will calls for trust and discipline, but it brings lasting and authentic freedom. At times, we may pray over a personal intention. It may not be a bad intention, but for some reason things are not working out. There is frustration. There are obstacles. We do not get what we want. Is God denying us something good? I have learned that denials can still serve God's will. I may send out several job applications to decent places of employment. I may be rejected by all of them and wonder why. I have prayed and I have asked for God's help. Later on, I discover that these rejections needed to happen so that I could be where God has called me to serve at a particular time and in a particular place. What we may perceive as denial may really be a delay so that we can be ready for the right place at the right time. Understanding God's will requires patience and humility. When we place ourselves in God's care, God will feed us with fish and not snakes. "No" as an answer to prayer, especially when it is rooted in God's will, may mean a few things: not now, or God has something better in mind, or this is not good for you. God's will helps us understand the answers we receive when we bring our heart's desires to prayer.

In October 2008, I lost a dear sister-in-law, Anita, to breast cancer. She was first diagnosed in 2001. She had a few good years between treatments, but the cancer spread in 2008 and she died soon after. As I was adding some finishing touches to this manuscript, I thought that I would like to say something about her. She was a loving wife and a devoted mother. Her family and friends rejoiced in her sweet and agreeable nature. She was known for saying, "Do the right thing." Whenever someone would go to her for advice about a conflict or some other issue, she would look that person in the eye and say, "Do the right thing." Having known her for eight years, I knew that doing the right thing for her meant "Do God's will." She had no malice and was sincere in her interactions with all people. She was distressed whenever there were misunderstandings. She was honest and truthful with everyone and encouraged all of us to put our egos aside and do what is right before our God. She embodied the golden rule and held no grudges. For her, doing God's will was second nature.

At times, we may know what God's will is for a particular situation, but pride and ego prevent us from making the right decision. We may say, "Not now" or "Why do I need to make the first move?" Someone we have not spoken to for years may be terminally ill and we are faced with a dilemma. We have not reconciled, but we know that visiting the person or offering to visit is the right thing to do. We may not find God's will easy, but truth cannot be denied. Life is too short to live with regret. Regret and anxiety are signs that we have missed an opportunity to "Do the right thing."

Reflection questions

- What is your understanding of God's will on earth?
- What are some obstacles that prevent you from doing God's will?

Prayer

Gracious God,

fear and pride can keep us from accepting and understanding your will.

We may become attached to thoughts, actions, and work that are unfulfilling and harmful.

Grant that, in humility, we may accept your will for us as you desire our healing and restoration.

Amen.

Give us this day our daily bread

Petition #4: *Give us this day our daily bread*

The "us" in this petition once again emphasizes the need to be in solidarity with each other in all things spiritual, political, physical, and social. Furthermore, "this day" speaks of the present-day implications of salvation.[19] God has great concern for our daily needs. A Human Development Report completed by a United Nations program noted that half of the world's population, nearly three billion people, lives on less than $2 per day.[20] The same report declared that nearly a billion people entered the 21st century unable to read a book or sign their names. Twenty percent of the population, living in the developed nations, consumes 86 percent of the world's goods. Approximately 790 million people in the developing world, almost two thirds of whom reside in Asia and the Pacific region, are still chronically undernourished. According to recent UNICEF findings, 30,000 children die each day due to poverty. Meanwhile, in Europe, $50 billion U.S. is spent on cigarettes every year. Europeans consume $105 billion U.S. in alcohol per year. This does not include the hundreds of billions of dollars that go into the sale of narcotics and military spending.[21]

In my own city of Hamilton, in Ontario, Canada, 14,200 households will put more than 50 percent of their household income toward rent; 4,306 families and individuals will spend another day on the active waiting list for subsidized housing. Three hundred and ninety-nine homeless men, women, and children will wake up in one of the city's emergency shelters. Two hundred and nineteen families or individuals will visit a food bank, and 150 people will receive a hot meal from a local charity.[22] These issues, which are not unique to Hamilton, call for greater community awareness. Clearly, the world's "bread" is not reaching all of God's children "this day."

What is "Daily Bread"?

The *Catechism of the Catholic Church* defines "daily bread" as "all appropriate goods and blessings, both material and spiritual" (CCC, 2830). For people to grow physically, emotionally, and spiritually, their basic human needs must be met. The official teaching of the Catholic Church goes on to affirm the universal need for human development and the sharing of "material resources" (*Ad Gentes*, 19). Salvation, then, must be concerned with the whole community. God desires to save the mind, the spirit, the body, the environment, and relationships. The Lord's Prayer reveals God's multiple concerns for the whole world. Jesus offers an understanding that takes into account the need for fulfillment in the present, and hope for perfect fulfillment in the future. In other words, he seems to be speaking of a certain type of restoration or making right of individuals and communities. This making right of communities involves deliverance from personal and social sin so that God's "daily bread" can reach us today. While we will speak of spiritual blessings throughout this book, in this section we will focus on the spiritual dimension of material blessings and human liberation.

In Luke's gospel, Jesus reads from a scroll of the prophet Isaiah: "The Spirit of the Lord is upon me, because he has anointed me to bring good news to the poor. He has sent me to proclaim release to the captives and recovery of sight to the blind, to let the oppressed go free, to proclaim the year of the Lord's favour" (Luke 4:18-19). In the same gospel, Mary proclaims, "He has brought down the powerful from their thrones, and lifted up the lowly, he has filled the hungry with good things, and sent the rich away empty" (Luke 1:52-53). God's will involves freedom, deliverance, and liberation. Liberation and deliverance are very much tied to salvation in the Hebrew Scriptures[23] and in the New Testament.[24] Jesus showed great concern for all people and fed them with his words and his ministry. In Mark's gospel, we hear an account of the feeding of the five thousand: "As he went ashore, he saw a great crowd; and he had compassion for them, because they were like sheep without a shepherd; and he began to teach them many things" (Mark 6:34). He fed them with his teaching, but he had compassion for them because they needed to eat. The disciples complained that there was not enough food to feed the crowd. "Taking the five loaves and the two fish, he looked up to heaven, and blessed and broke the loaves, and gave them to his disciples to set before the people; and he divided the two fish among them all. And all ate and were filled…" (Mark 6:41-42). The people needed both physical and spiritual nourishment.

As a mother, I have noticed first-hand in my children that hunger causes mood swings, an inability to concentrate, and irritability. Each morning, my youngest daughter, Beata, comes to my bed and the first words out of her mouth are "I'm hungry." Many elementary schools throughout North America have introduced breakfast programs so that children can be nourished before school starts. A good breakfast helps them be more alert and responsive. Jesus knew that our physical wants can distract us from learning and growing. The Second Vatican Council, too, spoke of the need to be liberated from all that prevents human fulfillment (see *Gaudium et Spes*, 12).

This call to solidarity with the suffering people of the world was reaffirmed by Pope Paul VI, who wrote, "the Church … has the duty to proclaim the liberation of millions of human beings, many of whom are her own children; the duty of assisting the birth of this liberation, of giving witness to it, of ensuring that it is complete" (*Evangelii Nuntiandi*, 30). Liberation is central to our discussion of what it means to save whole persons. Sin and salvation have spiritual, personal, communal, ecological, and political dimensions.

Men and women of different classes, races, and cultures have contributed their insights and lived experience to the way theology works within different social contexts. New voices have challenged systems of thought and deeds that prevent humanity from flourishing socially, economically, spiritually, and politically. People have different needs that must be met for them to survive: proper health care, education, shelter, food, a clean environment, or justice and freedom. Whenever basic human needs are not met, freedom is frustrated. People's sense of self may become weakened due to despair and discouragement. This despair can lead to self-loathing, which can have a negative effect on their world view, relationships, and choices.

Whenever we fail to see one another as created in the image and likeness of God, no matter what our gender, race, or creed, we frustrate God's plan to liberate us. Speaking about the God of life requires all people to work toward fulfillment, restoration, deliverance, and a process of humanization. Faith and hope can challenge dehumanizing situations.

Salvation, as we know, is a gift from God. We are called to participate actively in bringing this gift into the present. That is why we pray, "Your kingdom come. Your will be done, on earth as it is in heaven." We need to communicate the liberation and deliverance that God wills for God's people.

The desire to have basic needs met is universal. In different contexts and communities, we see a variety of struggles, but the desire to be delivered from pain unites all people. The need for liberation, as an essential step on the journey toward salvation, is expressed by people throughout the world. A Human Development Report completed by the United Nations Development Program found that 21.8 million adults and 830,000 children were infected with the HIV/AIDS virus in 1998.[25] Many of these cases were in Africa where resources and access to health care can be very limited. For some people, "daily bread" may mean access to health care and dignity in illness and death.

Here in Canada, the Canadian Conference of Catholic Bishops has addressed issues relating to labour unions, housing, citizenship, labour and immigration, poverty, social injustice, the distribution of the world's goods, development, employment, and Christian responsibility in social and political contexts.[26] "Christians in collaboration with fellow citizens have the continuing obligation of improving the quantity and quality of their social and political commitments," the bishops say.[27] We are called to identify and root out the underlying causes of poverty, homelessness, injustice, and violence.

This petition reminds us that God remains very interested in our affairs.

"Daily bread" signifies something that is needed to satisfy our hunger. Being of Italian descent, I was raised on bread and pasta. On days when we did not eat pasta or bread, I felt deprived. My mother would say, "Without pasta I feel dissatisfied, like something's missing." On those nights that pasta was not part of dinner, I would find myself searching through cupboards and the fridge for something else to eat. In cultures where bread or rice is the staple, people may feel dissatisfied if a meal does not include these foods. The present shortage of rice in some parts of the world should alarm us and remind us of the need to act on behalf of others. Their "daily bread" is being taken away from them. In the Lord's Prayer, we are dealing with the need for spiritual and material blessings. In July 2008, I heard of a bread shortage in Egypt. A mother of four waited in line from 7:00 a.m. until 2:00 p.m. for bread, only to be told that there was none left. She despaired and shared stories of people shooting each other for bread. We do not know the day or the hour when something like this may touch us. We must pray for the world's needy so that they may be delivered from this dreadful hour.

Jesus says, "I am the bread of life" (John 6:48). There is something about him that provides the spiritual staple of our lives. The one who satisfies spiritually is letting us know that he wants to provide for our basic needs. Human responsibility and a sense of social justice serve to bring this petition to fruition. Material blessing is part of the greater spiritual blessing. To be able to read and write, receive proper health care, be treated justly at work, and have the resources for survival, shelter, and food are all part of God's plan for us.

In the Acts of the Apostles, we are told that the apostles were concerned about the needs of the crowds. While they addressed the people's spiritual needs, they made sure that their physical needs were met as well: "There was not a needy person among them, for as many as owned lands or houses sold them and brought the proceeds of what was sold. They laid it at the apostles' feet, and it was distributed to each as any had need" (Acts 4:34-35). In the same way, Jesus travelled and preached to the crowds; he showed great concern for their spiritual and bodily needs. Before the miracle of the multiplication of the loaves, he says, "I have compassion for the crowd, because they have been with me now for three days and have nothing to eat; and I do not want to send them away hungry, for they might faint on the way" (Matthew 15:32). Jesus knows that we cannot function or learn without proper nourishment.

Our will to meet communal needs satisfies God's will for us to receive our "daily bread" and to love our neighbours. Our personal desires are universal desires. While this petition acknowledges our desire to have our daily needs met, it challenges us to trust: "this day." We ask for what we need "this day." While we do not know what lies in store for us tomorrow, we are called to trust that God will care for us. Jesus reminds us of this need to trust: "So do not worry about tomorrow, for tomorrow will bring worries of its own. Today's trouble is enough for today" (Matthew 6:34). This beautiful petition reminds us that God is concerned for our well-being and survival. In trusting God, we are called to act justly and serve the vulnerable.

We must not be passive in the face of need. The Letter of James reminds us of this truth: "Religion that is pure and undefiled before God, the Father, is this: to care for orphans and widows in their distress, and to keep oneself unstained by the world" (James 1:27).

We have been told what is good in the sight of the Lord: "to do justice, and to love with kindness, and to walk humbly with your God" (Micah 6:8). We do not know the day or the hour when we may be the vulnerable ones. When that day comes, our hope is that others will love us with kindness. We may have our "daily bread" today, but others depend on us to make sure they have the same. "If a brother or sister is naked and lacks daily food, and one of you says to them, 'Go in peace; keep warm and eat your fill', and yet you do not supply their bodily needs, what is the good of that?" (James 2:15-16).

Reflection questions

- What does your community teach about social justice?
- How does your community address the social needs of its members? Of people in other parts of the world?
- Think of ways you and your family can contribute to the cause of justice.

Prayer

*Compassionate God, you know our needs
before we give voice to them.*

*Grant that those people who need
physical and spiritual nourishment
may find mercy, generosity, and justice.*

*Show us how to care for one another,
as we are called to be generous with our gifts
and resources.*

We ask this through Christ our Lord.

Amen.

And forgive us our debts, as we also have forgiven our debtors

Petition #5: *And forgive us our debts, as we also have forgiven our debtors*

In his letter to the Romans, Paul writes, "Besides this, you know what time it is, how it is now the moment for you to wake from sleep. For salvation is nearer to us now than when we became believers; the night is far gone, the day is near" (Romans 13:11).

Once we have responded to God's call to save, the scriptures support us in turning away from all that prevents our fulfillment and in turning toward that which heals and liberates (Acts 3:19, 26, 5:31). This conversion or awakening is pleasing to God, as the "first work of the grace of the Holy Spirit is conversion ..." (*Catechism of the Catholic Church*, 1989). Before Jesus' ascension to God in heaven, Jesus opened the minds of the disciples so that they would understand the scriptures. He said to them, "Thus it is written, that the Messiah is to suffer and to rise from the dead on the third day, and that repentance and forgiveness of sins is to be proclaimed in his name to all nations, beginning from Jerusalem" (Luke 24:45-47). Jesus came to call sinners (Luke 5:32) and to "give knowledge of salvation to his people by the forgiveness of their sins" (Luke 1:77).

A desire for salvation can arise as a result of repentance: "Repent, for the kingdom of heaven has come near" (Matthew 4:17). The anonymous author of the mystical work *The Cloud of Unknowing* wrote, "labour and sweat to know one's true self, then and only then can one know God and salvation."[28] This statement suggests that, to know salvation, we need to do some work. This work involves knowledge of our weaknesses and sins, and requires us to understand and forgive ourselves and others. Forgiveness and understanding go hand in hand. This type of understanding, however, comes with humility and conversion. Once we learn more about ourselves—the way we respond to others, to stress, to pain and suffering—the more we understand others who go through the same experiences. Understanding brings mercy and makes it easier for us to forgive. Often, we may have trouble forgiving others because we cannot understand why they do or say certain things. Conversion, or turning away from unfulfilling habits, thoughts, and words, sets the process of understanding in motion.

Experiencing God through conversion is central to living and speaking of a life of fulfillment. Our encounter with God is reflected in our thoughts, words, and actions. Conversion leads to changes and spiritual developments. These changes and developments continue throughout our spiritual journey. As we revisit past mistakes and sins, our lives are transformed. We begin to see with new eyes, and to view ourselves, others, and God differently. This new way of seeing has personal, social, moral, and intellectual implications. Luke's account of the prodigal son (Luke 15:11-32), for example, shows how the son's repentance led him to reconcile with his father and restore everything he himself had lost. This parable is a great inspiration for parents and all people who are called to extend forgiveness. The story teaches them patience and offers hope as they wait for transformation.

The great message here is that once we have showed sincere sorrow, or contrition, the person granting forgiveness should not remind us of our sins. Once understanding has occurred, there is no need to revisit the past. Reminding people of their past, especially once they have repented, reshames them and sends a clear message that they are not forgiven. The father in the parable shows us how to minister to those who are "found," or no longer lost. The process of forgiveness brings healing to all involved. Those who have been hurt learn mercy; those who were lost are found. Parents may experience this process as their children go through the challenging teenage years. They may watch their children make bad choices that lead to pain. It may take years before these children see how their choices caused them and their families pain.

It is a great gift for parents to see their child turn away from destructive habits. It is an even greater gift for parents to see their child learn from mistakes. Here, the experience of repentance and conversion leads to transformation, reconciliation, and restoration. This process is not easy; it is easy to lose patience with the one who is lost. Bad habits are seductive and can become comfortable. At times, it may be easier to maintain the familiar, even if it is mediocre at best, destructive at worst. Those who are praying and waiting for change are called to be active yet merciful in their desire for change.

Jesus, who came to save the lost, gives us many examples of waiting and hope. His desire to bring about reconciliation in people and communities is evident in the story of the woman caught in adultery (John 8:1-11). In this story, we hear that the scribes and the Pharisees brought "a woman who had been caught in adultery; and making her stand before all of them, they said to him [Jesus], 'Teacher, this woman was caught in the very act of committing adultery. Now in the law Moses commanded us to stone such women. Now what do you say?'" Jesus challenges the crowd to reconsider their own actions and sins before proceeding: "Let anyone among you who is without sin be the first to throw a stone at her." Note that he does not say, "Let anyone among you who has not committed adultery be the first to throw a stone at her." This is an important distinction, as Jesus was making a point about judgment.

One person's weakness may be infidelity; another's may be greed; another's may be an abusive tongue or actions; yet another may be the town gossip or a compulsive liar. At times, we may be tempted to judge someone who has a different weakness from our own. We may attack weakness with judgment. Yet one person's weakness may not be a struggle for another person. Lack of understanding and of life experience may lead us to judge. Jesus reminds us that we need to be compassionate. He is, however, firm in his call to conversion: "Go your way, and from now on do not sin again."

Conversion is a long and challenging process, but the fruit it bears is long-lasting and transforming. Some people may confuse conversion with a response to God's call. A response to God occurs in a moment, but living out that response takes a lifetime. Many people who have thriving ministries have years of life experience; their life lessons are joy and pain. Time alone separates a student from the teacher. It takes time for humility and trust to take root. In becoming a new person, we are given a new personality. This gradual restructuring of our personality is part of the process of salvation and the forgiveness of sins. In this process of spiritual transformation, we begin to feel free and fulfilled. This process of reintegration shows us how our habits, thoughts, and sins have prevented God's light from shining through. Our integration happens through self-knowledge, repentance, understanding, and growth. This self-knowledge, repentance, and growth will give us the understanding we need to forgive ourselves and others, to heal, and to move forward with our spiritual growth. As we open ourselves to God's parenting guidance, God will show us how to see ourselves and others. When we see others as God sees them, we have some understanding into how and why people act as they do.

Here we may see conversion as a return to the original state in which human beings were created. God's image is restored in us. Christ restores people by healing them, finding them when they are lost, freeing them from their unfulfilling desires, and forgiving them their sins. The struggle of repentance and forgiveness is part of the journey toward salvation.

Sin, or a turning away from God in thought and action, frustrates freedom and puts limits on wellness, healing, and the attainment of truth. Sin brings us to a lower state and discourages us from attaining the wholeness we are called to achieve. Repentance and forgiveness move us to consider the implications of our choices. Lack of forgiveness toward oneself can lead to feelings of shame, guilt, low self-esteem, and self-loathing. Lack of forgiveness toward others can lead to grudges, rage, and hardness of heart. In responding to God's desire to save us, we must cooperate by saving ourselves from our own demons. Forgiveness, however, does not imply allowing ourselves to be abused or exploited. We are called to be patient and understanding when supporting truth; however, when faced with error or falsehood, we are called to correct one another in the spirit of Christ. The gift of understanding will help us discern so we can recognize situations that lead to destruction and unfulfilling relationships and can help the person become free of these by forgiving him or her.

Knowledge of God's desire to make us whole leads to a greater understanding of our need for conversion and forgiveness. Humility and repentance are the foundations for this step. We are open to receive God's mercy and be set free to love with no unhealthy ties to our past. There is no room for pride and perfectionism, as these vices can limit growth and cause frustration. God is merciful and calls us to be merciful toward ourselves (Matthew 22:27-40). Salvation involves a "yes" to God's offer and to our openness to be made well and to acknowledge our faults and sins. God knows all that prevents freedom and fulfillment and will show us what we need to abandon so that God's grace can work in us. Jesus' message and ministry bring us back to God and prompt us to reconcile with one another. Jesus' life and death bring about the forgiveness of sins. The Resurrection of Jesus is the greatest gift to humanity, as it confirms that all that is lost can be restored; all sin can be forgiven: new life can emerge through hope in healing. Our pain can be vindicated. What may appear as a hopeless situation can be redeemed. Forgiveness heals our understanding of ourselves. The person we are at 40 is not the person we were at 10, 20, or even 30. The person we are at 70 will not be the same as who we were at 40 or 50. With prayer, self-understanding, and spiritual growth, we should become more fulfilled, more understanding, and more compassionate. Without these efforts, healing can be blocked due to hardness of heart and pride.

Some people do not want to see past their own pain and limited understanding. They project their flawed ideas onto others and blame others for their misfortune and pain. They fail to see how their own behaviour contributes to their own struggles. It is difficult to minister to such people. We can pray for them and offer our help, but God needs their cooperation. We cannot give understanding to people. We can model forgiveness and mercy, but a hard heart is difficult to soften. For those of us who desire reconciliation or healing in relationships, we must be patient and trust in God's providence. We cannot feel responsible for one person's lack of response toward God. Some people learn from other people's mistakes, but some need to learn from their own life experience.

Whenever I am asked to speak about the connection between understanding and forgiveness, I use the following analogy. A teenage girl worked in a variety store for a year. During that year, she and another employee learned how to manipulate the cash register so that they could steal money on a weekly basis. Eventually, her employer let her go. The girl was offered a job in another store, but she declined and found a job where she did not have access to money. She did well in this job and did not steal again. At age 23, she began to worship at a local church. During this time, she reflected on her past actions. In the sacrament of Reconciliation, she confessed her past sin of theft. While she admitted that what she did was wrong, she did not understand why she had stolen. The priest assured her of God's forgiveness and she received God's grace. Little did she know that in time, this grace would lead her to the understanding she needed. Forgiveness is assured, but God wants to give us understanding as well so that our learning can be complete. This understanding is connected to our desire to restore what has been lost or distorted. Offering satisfaction for our sins is our way of showing through thought, word, and action that we desire restoration of balance in our lives.

The young woman, now married with three children, runs her own business. The business is taking her away from her family, so she decides to hire a teenage boy to work on weekends. After a few months, she discovers that money has gone missing, but cannot prove that the teenage employee is responsible. She is discouraged, as she was short in her monthly income and was unable to cover some bills. In this moment, she is given full understanding and clarity about her choice to steal as a teenager. She sees the damage that she did by denying the money to its proper owner. But the understanding does not end here. She has renewed mercy toward herself as she looks back and realizes that as a teenager, she did not know the implications of her choices. She stole because it was easy. She did not mean to hurt anyone and did not know that anyone would suffer. She then looked at this young man and thought, "Does he know what he is doing?" Recall Jesus on the cross: "Father, forgive them; for they do not know what they are doing" (Luke 23:34). If we knew all the consequences of our actions before we did them, our choices would be different. The problem is that understanding is not always present.

Psychologists who study adolescent brain development tell us that teenage brains are still under construction. They do not understand risk the way adults do.

In the above story, the woman's process of forgiveness and healing has come full circle. While the boy's actions were wrong, they taught her something about herself and about this boy. Without this experience, she might have gone through life hating a part of herself, wondering how she could have stolen. Even though God had forgiven her, she was having a hard time forgiving herself. For many of us, forgiveness and understanding may take years of life experience, humility, and prayer.

In our quest to evangelize and teach about Jesus, we are called to lifelong conversion and understanding of forgiveness. Jesus' words in the gospel of Luke are relevant. Recall his words before the ascension: "Thus it is written, that the Messiah is to suffer and to rise from the dead on the third day, and that repentance and forgiveness of sins is to be proclaimed in his name to all nations, beginning from Jerusalem" (Luke 24:46-47). The key words here are "beginning from Jerusalem." This phrase implies that we need to clean up our own house before we offer advice to others. We need to bring healing and forgiveness to our own families and communities. Also, Matthew's gospel reminds us that Jesus "will save his people from their sins" (Matthew 1:21). Throughout the gospels, Jesus challenges the people in his community to repent and to do God's will. Interpreted for today, this approach suggests the need for in-house evangelization or the conversion of baptized Christians. The official teaching of the Catholic Church calls all Christians to "interior conversion" (See *Unitatis Redintegratio*, 7, and *Lumen Gentium*, 14). While the book of Acts encourages the spread of the gospel to the Gentiles—"And they praised God, saying, 'Then God has given even to the Gentiles the repentance that leads to life'" (Acts 11:18)—Jesus wants his mission to be made known to his community first (Luke 24:47). The gift of salvation is relevant only when it is lived; preaching the gift of salvation is not enough. How can Christians communicate the gift of the forgiveness of sins if they do not believe it or experience it themselves? The Church is in need of credible witnesses. Jesus knew that the members of his own community had greater need of his message. The believers of his day may have believed they knew all there was to know about following God, but John the Baptist, like Jesus, proves otherwise: "Do not begin to say to yourselves, 'We have Abraham as our ancestor'; for I tell you, God is able from these stones to raise up children to Abraham" (Luke 3:7-9). We cannot make any assumptions about our spiritual state based on our religious heritage.

The words "beginning in Jerusalem" should inspire Christians as they seek to do God's will and be saved. Jesus calls for awareness and conversion within each person's own tradition, or else "the kingdom of God will be taken away from you and given to a people that produces the fruits of the kingdom" (Matthew 21:43). Following Jesus' warning, Christians are to reconsider their need for repentance and forgiveness. Some Christians, in their ambitious desire to preach the gospel to members of other religions, may lose sight of their own need for conversion. Some people may be more interested in seeing salvation than in reading or hearing about it. Some people may feel forced to follow the precepts of their own Christian traditions out of obligation rather than love. Some Christians may be preaching an experience of which they have little knowledge to a group of people who may be living it each day in their own traditions. If Christians live their salvation, then, and only then, will the Church be a sign or "universal sacrament of salvation" to others. We cannot be this sacrament without the process of conversion. We cannot be made whole without the process of conversion. Healing is the fruit of forgiveness and understanding.

Repentance and the forgiveness of sins lead to healing and restoration. The gospels tells us of several miracles of healing that are linked to the forgiveness of sins: for example, Mark 2:1-12 and John 5:1-4, where a sick man was made well and told not to sin anymore. The healing of the paralyzed man reveals an important connection between emotional healing and sin:

> And after getting into a boat he crossed the sea and came to his own town. And just then some people were carrying a paralyzed man lying on a bed. When Jesus saw their faith, he said to the paralytic, "Take heart, son; your sins are forgiven." Then some of the scribes said to themselves, "This man is blaspheming." But Jesus, perceiving their thoughts, said, "Why do you think evil in your hearts? For which is easier to say, 'Your sins are forgiven,' or to

say 'Stand up and walk'? But so that you may know that
the Son of Man has authority on earth to forgive sins"—
he then said to the paralytic—"Stand up, take your bed
and go to your home." (Matthew 9:1-9)

This is an exciting passage as it makes a connection
between the faith of a community, the need for forgiveness,
and healing. Jesus knew that this man needed more than the
words "stand up and walk." While in other healing accounts
Jesus praises the faith of the sick and says, "your faith has
made you well [saved you]" (Mark 10:52), in Matthew's account of the paralyzed man, did Jesus imply that the man's
sins, or his holding on to shame and guilt, had caused his
illness? I believe that the man's need to be delivered from
shame and guilt was met with these words of Jesus: "your
sins are forgiven." While the faith of the community inspired Jesus, he knew something else was needed for this
man to be made well. For me, Jesus is communicating
something powerful. Could it be that repressed feelings of
shame, resentment and guilt can make us ill? Here Jesus is
healing the whole person, not just the body. Jesus healed
this man's paralysis, but the healing went deeper. This man's
mind, memory, and soul were healed as he was released
from the burden of his past experiences. Some people may
find themselves emotionally paralyzed due to feelings of
shame and guilt. Today, the connection between negative
emotion and health has inspired some healthcare profes-
sionals to reconsider their approach to healing.

Health and Forgiveness

In 1974, Dr. M. T. Morter, a chiropractor practicing in Arkansas, began developing a new chiropractic procedure called the Bio Energetic Synchronization Technique (B.E.S.T.). This method identifies and removes any psychological interferences that *may* cause illness. B.E.S.T. addresses how memory, negative emotion, and guilt may cause illness. In his book *The Soul Purpose*, he writes, "In my clinical experience, I have encountered many traumatic situations with a myriad of patients over the years. It is not necessary to agree with the person or the event, but it is imperative to your health that you forgive …."[29] He goes on to suggest that to forgive does not mean to condone; however, he notes, harbouring grudges and anger prevents people from getting well. Forgiveness of self and others, meanwhile, leads to improved health. While many illnesses, especially those afflicting the young, remain a mystery and a test of faith, some research supports the claim that stress and emotional duress can weaken the immune system. Of course this is not true of all illnesses, and I do not wish to suggest that people are entirely responsible for every illness. Saying that all illnesses can be blamed on negative emotions would be untrue, inappropriate and insensitive. Some physicians have found, though, that there is a connection between health and forgiveness. As St. James wrote, "The prayer of faith will save the sick, and the Lord will raise them up; and anyone who has committed sins will be forgiven. Therefore confess your sins to one another, so that you may be healed. The prayer of the righteous is powerful and effective" (James 5:15-16).

Today, doctors admit that there is a physiological reason why emotions affect health. "Now physicians talk about the role the mind plays in cancer, in arthritis, and yes, in migraines."[30] According to James P. Henry, different parts of the brain are associated with specific emotions. The release of certain emotions is associated with different emotional responses; the hormones released with those emotions affect health.[31] The field of study that investigates this connection between emotion and the immune system is psychoneuroimmunology: the "scientific investigation of how the brain affects the body's immune cells and how the immune system can be affected by behaviour …."[32] The term "psychoneuroimmunology" was coined in 1964 by Dr. Robert Ader.[33]

> In their landmark study, Ader and his colleagues showed that immune function could be classic[al]ly conditioned. The science of psychoneuroimmunology focuses on the links between the mind, the brain, and the immune system, with an intricate interaction of consciousness, brain and central nervous system, and the immune system. As a science, it has received the endorsement of National Institutes of Health.[34]

These same researchers note that more than 4,000 years ago, Chinese healers found that frustration and negative emotion often caused physical illness.[35] It is interesting that 2,000 years after them, Jesus continued to make the connection between emotion and health (Matthew 9:1-8).

Today, doctors and researchers have evidence that the body's levels of immunity can be influenced by stress. Stress "and other psychological factors make the body more susceptible to infectious diseases, autoimmune diseases, or cancer."[36] The American Cancer Society revealed that, in 2002, there were 10.9 million new cases of cancer worldwide. In 2006, the same source noted that nearly 1.4 million people will be diagnosed with cancer in the United States. Again, while we cannot know the cause of all illnesses, some research does show that guilt, shame, and lack of forgiveness may compromise a person's health: "Essential to a spiritual nature is forgiveness—the ability to release from the mind all the past hurts and failures, all sense of guilt and loss …, forgiveness enables one to banish resentment."[37]

Forgiveness, for Dr. Joan Borysenko, is "accepting the core of every human being as the same as yourself and giving them the gift of not judging them."[38] Some psychologists estimate that at least seven of every ten people carry throughout their lives feelings of guilt and shame—feelings of having committed a sin or mistake for which they have never been forgiven.[39] This lingering sense of shame or guilt can be harmful; doctors have noted the physical effects of lack of forgiveness toward oneself or others:

> The body manufactures masses of "high-voltage" chemicals, like adrenaline, non-adrenaline, adrenocorticotrophic hormone and cortisone. When too many of these high-voltage chemicals build up in the bloodstream, a person becomes a rapidly ticking time bomb, a prime

candidate for some specific ills such as tension-vascular headaches. The heart pounds like a sledgehammer in the chest; the muscles in the neck and shoulders start to contract; abdominal pains develop. If the situation continues unchecked, gastric ulcers, gastritis, or irritable bowel syndrome can result. With forgiveness, the anger and resentment dissolve. The body stops pouring high-voltage chemicals into the bloodstream. The healing begins.[40]

Perhaps Jesus was practising psychoneuroimmunology in his ministry. Aware of the connection between forgiveness and health, he preached the need to be healed from guilt and shame. In this process of healing, however, we must never be tempted to think of illness as a punishment from God. Rather, we should start "thinking about God as healer, the Almighty, the Good Shepherd, [our] Redeemer, and [our] Saviour."[41] The healing of a man born blind confirms this point: "As he [Jesus] walked along, he saw a man born blind from birth. His disciples asked him, 'Rabbi, who sinned, this man or his parents, that he was born blind?' Jesus answered, 'Neither this man nor his parents sinned; he was born blind so that God's works might be revealed in him" (John 9:1-3). Jesus goes on to heal this man. Jesus challenges the views of those who equate all illness with past sins. The diverse healings Jesus performed show that illness has many different causes.

Today we know that environmental pollution can cause illness. While many causes of illness remain a mystery, it is clear that some may be due to or made worse by stress and emotional pain. For Jesus, the need to be delivered from personal sin and grudges was part of the process of salvation, or being made well:

> To Jesus, "health" meant much more than the absence of sickness. It meant the wholeness of God …. We will find that health is the wholeness of God, a wholeness we are called to when we become sharers in the divine nature. We grow into God's own health as we allow his friendship to transform our patterns of human behavior at every level of our being—mind, will, emotions and even bodily functions.[42]

Understanding health as something that involves the whole person can help us make the connections between thoughts, deeds, and health. "Holiness" requires "wholeness" and healing of the whole person. A person may appear "well," but may be paralyzed with rage. Another person may "appear" unwell, but may be more "whole" than the one who appears "well." It is not unusual for people who are struggling with a physical illness to undergo some type of emotional healing. The body may remain unwell, but the sick person is transformed and his or her loved ones are changed. Different levels of healing occur during times of struggle. One person's bodily illness may heal another person emotionally. I have seen people who were hard and unapproachable become soft and compassionate through their own struggle or through the struggle of someone they love.

Various ministries have been created to help people who are suffering due to shame or guilt to find healing. In my own diocese of Hamilton, I have seen how prison ministry and ministries for separated and divorced people have brought healing and hope to those in need of reconciliation. More recently, several dioceses throughout North America have embraced a ministry of healing and reconciliation called "Project Rachel," which ministers to women and men who have suffered due to the termination of a pregnancy. Through providing confidential support and counselling, this ministry has helped many who need to be set free from past experiences. As a former high school and university chaplain, I can recall numerous moments where people felt liberated and healed after they were forgiven and they repented. This deliverance, however, means accepting forgiveness from God, ourselves, and others (Matthew 6:9-13). If we are plagued with a false sense of self because we cannot let go of these negative experiences in our past, forgiveness can set us free to love ourselves, others, and God more completely, and can offer us healing of body, mind, and spirit.

A deeper understanding of the complexity of the human person can teach people how to make connections between how suppressed emotions affect their health. Suppressed emotions do not disappear when we cover them up; we must address and process them if we want to be free of them. Healing can happen once we face difficult feelings. More dialogue is needed between Christians and scientists: "… church leaders often seem to be out of step with new scientific findings, and run the risk of attacking scientific perspectives without fully understanding the facts," says Dr. Francis S. Collins, head of the Human Genome Project (the study of DNA) and one of the world's leading scientists.[43] Quoting the Book of Proverbs, he reminds people of faith that "it is not good to have zeal without knowledge" (Proverbs 19:2). To learn more about how the mind may influence the body, and to see how co-operating with God's healing grace can heal us, Christians need to be in dialogue with those experts who can support our claims with scientific evidence. We, in turn, can inspire scientists to re-evaluate their religious beliefs. This exciting new dialogue, which can promote greater healing among all people, deserves our attention.

Reflection questions

- What is your understanding of forgiveness?
- Does it help you to see forgiveness as a process?
- Which areas in your life need more understanding?
- What do you think about the connection between health and emotions?

Prayer

Healing God,

some people may be plagued with thoughts of shame, regret, resentment, and anger.

Show us how to begin the process of forgiveness and healing.

Give us understanding, mercy, and wisdom as we seek to remove all obstacles to healing.

We ask this through Christ our Lord.

Amen.

And do not bring us to the time of trial

Petition #6: And do not bring us to the time of trial

This petition addresses the ever-present challenge of trials of all kinds. Today, we think of the various temptations that create trial and adversity: temptation in human relationships, temptation to commit crimes, temptation to cheat, temptation to betray, temptation to lie, temptation to gossip, temptation to fear, temptation to steal, temptation to abuse, temptation to consume substances that harm, and temptation to engage in activities that frustrate human freedom and fulfillment. One 2007 U.S. Census Bureau source on crime statistics in the U.S. noted that one murder is committed every 22 minutes, one rape every five minutes, one robbery every 49 seconds, one burglary every 10 seconds; also, the arrest rate of teens for murder had jumped 92 percent since 1985.[44] Similarly, Drug Rehabilitation Centers Services in the U.S.

found that by the late 1980s, 30 million people in North America were cocaine users, and six million were cocaine addicts.[45] In Canada, according to 2007 statistics, there were 101,000 drug offenses, 30,000 robberies nation-wide, and 111 homicides in Toronto alone.[46] Some of these crimes, however, may be related to drug use.

A person's sense of self, no matter what their religious affiliation, can be distorted due to abuse, oppression, violence, poverty, illness, and addiction. These and other painful experiences present times of "trial" or temptation for many people. As there is not space to explore each of these moments of "trial," I will address the need to be rescued from the globalization of addiction. Addiction is a "time of trial" that affects individuals, families, and communities; it has global implications. It may begin as a moment of weakness, as a response to stress, or as a way to cope with pain, or may be a product of a person's upbringing and genetic history:

> There is an inescapable component of heritability to many human behavioral traits. For virtually none of them is heredity ever close to predictive. Environment, particularly childhood experiences, and the prominent role of individual free will choices have a profound effect on us. Scientists will discover an increasing level of molecular detail about the inherited factors that undergird our personalities, but that should not lead us to overestimate their quantitative contribution. Yes, we have all been dealt a particular set of cards, and the cards will eventually be revealed. But how we play the hand is up to us.[47]

A 2004 Canadian survey on addictions reported that half of an individual's susceptibility to addiction is inherited, while the other half is the product of a person's environment—pressures of family, peers, and neighbourhood. Someone may have an inherited predisposition to addiction, but may be saved from it through a healthy home life and environment. Another person, raised in a stressful environment, may be tempted to pursue this inherited tendency.

About 13.6 percent of all Canadians are considered high-risk drinkers. About one in 20 Canadians reports a cannabis-related problem. The most commonly used illegal drug is hallucinogens, followed by cocaine, speed, and ecstasy. Self-reported rates of illegal drug use are increasing in Canada: the rate of self-reported use of cocaine rose from 3.5 percent in 1989, to 3.8 percent in 1994, to 10.6 percent in 2004. The rate of self-reported use of LSD/speed/heroin rose from 4.1 percent in 1989, to 5.9 percent in 1994, to 13.2 percent in 2004. The same Canadian Addictions Survey showed that the number of Canadians who report having used an injectable drug at some point in their life increased from 1.7 million in 1994 to over 4.1 million in 2004. Clearly, addiction, which destroys lives and devastates families, is a growing concern. Families who have gone through this chaos report feeling trapped and held hostage by loved ones who lie, cheat, and steal their way through an addiction. The whole family struggles to save their loved one. They must make difficult decisions to encourage their addicted loved one to get help.

Jesus spoke of attachments and the need to be delivered from them in order to gain eternal life (Matthew 19:16-22). Addiction is a global example of the world's need for healing and rehabilitation. Several scholars who have studied the spiritual dimension of addiction have called for a renewed understanding of healing and reconciliation among people with addictions. While professional therapeutic help is a big part of healing, scholars also speak of the need for God's grace and deliverance. Christian therapists have found that through a sincere surrender to God's healing grace and Jesus' example, people with addictions have been able to make stronger recoveries.

Conversion and trust in God lead many addicts to gain a restored sense of self. This restored sense of self is a key part of the healing process because addictions can, as physician Gerald May has found, distort one's relationship with God.[48] Dr. May defines addiction as "a state of compulsion, obsession, or preoccupation that enslaves a person's will and desire."[49] He observes that addictions generally have five characteristics: tolerance, withdrawal symptoms, self-deception, loss of willpower, and distortion of attention.[50] Stress coupled with an addiction can lead to an impaired sense of judgment and lack of reasoning ability. Weakness and moments of stress can lead a person to develop an unhealthy attachment, such as to people, work, habits, material belongings, or substances. In some cases, these attachments are placed before one's relationship with others and with God.

When I worked as a campus minister, I found that, for people with an addiction, their sense of peace and security depended on whether their addiction was satisfied. The addiction became the desired end. When addiction to a substance is physiological, the results can be catastrophic. In recent studies on brain chemistry and addictions, researchers found that brain chemistry changes as a result of an addiction. In alcoholics, for example, both the brain and the liver are affected. Addiction impedes right judgment, as the brain is no longer the same. The brain remembers and the body craves the substance. That is why relapses are common. And it's not just substances that cause these kinds of changes: studies show that gambling has the same effect on brain chemistry that substance addiction does.[51] Often, the need to satisfy these desires is placed before the wellness of the self, leaving people enslaved to their desires. As long as they are enslaved, their sense of self can never be healthy and true, just distorted and damaged. Addictions take away our ability to reason; the good news is that we can be delivered from our weaknesses (Romans 6:14-23). Desires can be good; but we must choose desires using reason.

The problem with reckless desire is that we may pursue things, people, habits, substances, and occupations that are unhealthy. The correct use of emotions and desires, on the other hand, is morally good, because these lead to the fulfillment of life. When we lose sight of God as our desired end, we move away from the fullness of life that God wants for us. God's love and grace can help us to pursue our appetites with reason. God's love and the correct use of our desires are necessary steps in the journey toward wellness.

The first step we must take is to ask God for help: in other words, we need to admit weakness.

In his work on addiction and grace, Dr. Gerald May has challenged people to consider the help of God's grace when addressing the psychological and physiological dynamics of addiction. The petition "And do not bring us to the time of trial" reminds us of our need for humility and surrender to God's guidance. We need to admit weakness before we can face any temptation. Pride causes us to give in to a temptation. We trick ourselves into thinking we are in control. "I can handle this." "I would never cheat on my spouse." "I will not get addicted." "Nothing is going to happen to me." "I'll do it once." "I can control myself and my urges." A call for God's grace can help us resist temptation. In the same way, God's grace can help us climb out of a potentially destructive habit. We must challenge all unhealthy attachments in our lives, as they can lead to addiction. In Dr. May's words, the "only effective way of ending an addictive behaviour is to stop it."[52] However, "grace is our only hope in dealing with addiction."[53] The trouble is that "the brain never completely forgets what it has learned."[54] Here we are struggling with our own physiology, for addiction affects physiology, mood, behaviour, and thoughts. So how do we break free from such attachments?

Dr. May notes that we never completely overcome our attachments. What we can do, he suggests, is turn to the grace of God to deliver us from bondage to them.[55] Grace is a supernatural free gift that gives us strength. Grace helps us to stay vigilant, as addiction can limit human freedom: "God creates us for love and freedom, attachment hinders us, and grace is necessary for salvation."[56] God must be our primary desire, as God's love and grace bring freedom and the right ordering of our desires. In my experience as a chaplain, I have seen a difference in people who surrender to God's offer of help. Professional counselling, humility, the ability to admit weakness, surrender, and God's grace can prevent people from being brought to the time of trial and, even if they temporarily have trials, God's grace can pull them out of difficulty. The problem, of course, is that we cannot force people to surrender. We can pray for them; we can offer assistance and guidance, but we cannot choose health for them. God honours each person's free will and waits for him or her to surrender and respond.

I remember watching a faith-related television show where the host interviewed a father and daughter. The father shared how he despaired for years as his daughter pursued a nasty drug habit and dated an abusive man. The father and his wife would go for months at a time, not hearing from their daughter. In their pain, they turned to God and asked for two things: that God would protect her and that God would get her attention. After years of prayer, she "woke up" and returned to her father's house. His story gives hope to all parents who are waiting for their children to return. Addiction robs us of our loved ones and turns our lives upside down. At times, God alone can give us comfort.

The story of the Samaritan woman in John's gospel carries us beyond the human desire to be fulfilled by people, habits, and substances. In this story, Jesus asks the Samaritan woman for a drink from a well. She complains that the well is deep and there is no bucket. He compares the water from the well with the "living water" that he gives: "Everyone who drinks of this water will be thirsty again, but those who drink of the water that I will give them will never be thirsty" (John 4:13-14). The woman is intrigued; she asks for some of this water. Instead, Jesus tells her to call her husband and then come back. We later discover that Jesus knew that she has had five husbands (John 4:18). Could Jesus be using the symbol of water from the well to describe the way this woman had been trying to satisfy her need for love through men? He tells her that she will continue to be thirsty if she drinks from the well, but if she allows Jesus to satisfy her needs with "living water" she may no longer need the well. Was Jesus telling her that for years she had turned to men to fulfill her? That she was addicted to relationships? That she was dependent on men to satisfy all her needs? That, if she continued to look to men to satisfy her needs, she would continue to be thirsty? I believe the answer to these questions is yes. While pastors will approach this text with different insights and life lessons, one could substitute any addiction in the place of the woman's husbands and see how Jesus is communicating something powerful about the love he offers.

When we find it hard to manage life's stresses, we may turn to habits and substances to help us cope. We may turn to unfulfilling relationships. The fulfillment the Samaritan woman is seeking does not come from a physical place or from a person; it comes from God through Jesus Christ.

Scientists have shown how addictions affect the pleasure centre of the brain. Once a craving has been satisfied, the brain tells the body that it needs more, only to be dissatisfied once the "high" passes. One dose, one completed activity such as gambling, is not enough. This does not mean that all relationships or habits are unhealthy; rather, it reminds us that it is unrealistic to place all of our needs on the shoulders of one person, or on a substance, a habit, or an occupation. The story of the Samaritan woman suggests that God is willing to offer us something that will satisfy us forever. One person, one habit, one job, one substance, can never fulfill such a promise.

Everyone needs deliverance from personal sin and unhealthy attachment. God desires to free all people from everything that enslaves them. St. Paul writes that he "will not be dominated by anything" (1 Corinthians 6:12); before he can reach this state of freedom, he must become aware of his weaknesses. He writes, "I do not understand my own actions. For I do not do what I want, but I do the very thing I hate" (Romans 7:15). Self-discipline is a process that requires hope and God's grace: "Without victory over self, there can be no rationality, no belief, no salvation. If man does not rule his passions, he is inevitably ruled by them."[57] Deliverance from all that harms the whole person is a key step in our journey to salvation. Freedom from unhealthy habits and attachments is for members of all religious traditions. Individuals are called to know "the fullness of grace and truth" (*Redemptoris Hominis*, 18) as it leads to inner transformation.

Pope John Paul II observed that people today seem to be under "threat from what [they] produce" with the work of their hands, their intellects, and their wills (*Redemptoris*

Hominis, 15). People have been challenged to consider the "exploitation of the earth" (*Redemptoris Hominis*, 15), the pollution of the human body, and the violation of human rights (*Redemptoris Hominis*, 17). This "time of trial" has widespread implications as we attempt to address all temptations that frustrate God's plan for our salvation.

Reflection questions

- How do you understand temptation?
- What has been your "time of trial"? How did you find your way through it?
- What are the spiritual implications of addiction?

Prayer

God of strength,

St. Paul reminds us of the importance of remaining humble and disciplined.

Give us the insight, hope, and patience we need to face times of trial.

Grant that we may cooperate with your grace as we strive to be made whole.

We ask this through Christ our Lord.

Amen.

Rescue us from the evil one

Petition #7: **Rescue us from the evil one**

For Christians, Jesus manifests God's will to deliver us from harm and danger. The concept of deliverance or being rescued is used throughout the New Testament. For St. Paul, deliverance is tied to freedom offered through Jesus Christ. In his letter to the Galatians, he writes, "For freedom Christ has set us free; stand fast, therefore, and do not submit again to a yoke of slavery" (Galatians 5:1). Further along, in the same letter, he declares that Christ has liberated people from bondage to the law (Galatians 5:1-12). This means that actions do not always indicate inner conversion. Once we move from doing something out of obligation to doing something out of love, God's law has become part of us. In Romans, St. Paul speaks of liberation from sin (Romans 6:14-23), and in 1 Corinthians, he says people are liberated from death (1 Corinthians 15). Liberation, however, is not limited to individual human life. It has cosmic implications as well: "creation itself will be set free from its bondage to decay and obtain the glorious liberty of the children of God" (Romans 8:21).

I was once asked to sum up St. Paul's teaching on deliverance and following the law. I use the following explanation on moral and spiritual development to explain his teachings. When we are toddlers, we are ignorant of how our actions affect others. I call this the "I do not know any better" phase. As we grow up, our parents and teachers show us how to follow directions and obey certain rules. The use of reason enters the picture. We are aware of these rules, but we may not understand them or the logic behind them. We may follow them out of a sense of obligation or because we do not want to get in trouble. This phase is the "I should know better" phase. We may get into trouble, but we have a sense of right and wrong. Our conscience drives our feelings of remorse or satisfaction. Or we may do certain things because someone or some authority has told us that doing these things is beneficial. Not doing them, then, may make us feel guilty. Fully mature Christians, however, evolve to a new phase: "I do know better." Here, they are aware of the consequences of wrong, but avoid evil because they love God. They follow God not so much out of a sense of duty or obligation, but, rather, out of love for God. Love drives their thoughts and actions. It would be painful not to do God's will. While rules are in place, fully mature Christians choose God's will no matter what. They understand the logic behind the teachings and are liberated from their own unfulfilling desires, as they are interested in doing God's will only. This is the liberation to which we are called. The ideal is to reach this level of understanding. It can be a difficult process, as there is an ongoing struggle between being pulled to do our will and accepting God's will.

Jesus Christ offers the message of liberation and salvation to all people. Whole persons in communities need to be saved from all that endangers them. *Gaudium et Spes*, a document from the Second Vatican Council, deals with this salvation of the whole person. The preface to this document emphasizes that the message of salvation is intended for all people. Since it is the human being who "must be saved" and "renewed," it is the human being "who is key to this discussion, the human being considered whole and entire, with body and soul, heart and conscience, mind and will" (*Gaudium et Spes*, 3). It is clear that human fulfillment involves the whole person. The whole person is called to seek what is good through the gift of freedom (*Gaudium et Spes*, 17). Furthermore, this document is rooted in Christ.

It seems it is affirming that Jesus is the example of what it means to be a saved human being:

> In reality it is only in the mystery of the Word made flesh that the mystery of man truly becomes clear. For Adam, the first man, was a type of him who was to come, Christ the Lord. Christ the new Adam, in the very revelation of the mystery of the Father and of his love, fully reveals man to himself and brings to light his most high calling. It is no wonder, then, that all the truths mentioned so far should find in him their source and their most perfect embodiment. (*Gaudium et Spes*, 22)

Jesus is presented as the "perfect man" who restores in us our likeness to God (*Gaudium et Spes*, 22; see also *Redemptoris Hominis*, 1, 13, 18). "He is the image of the invisible God, the firstborn of all creation" (Colossians 1:15). He raises our dignity as human beings and through him God unites Godself to each person: "God's being and man's have been conjoined."[58]

The fulfillment of humanity is part of God's plan, and Jesus is the "new man" (see *Redemptoris Hominis*, 18) to whom we are to look as the model of our true state. All human beings are called to this destiny. The pursuit of this common destiny requires hope and humility. The journey toward deliverance from personal and social sin is not an easy one: we are called to challenge and expose the evil that surrounds us.

Who or what is the "evil one"?

This petition asks God to protect us from the "evil one." In his prayer in John's gospel, Jesus repeats this request: "… I ask you to protect them [the disciples] from the evil one" (John 17:15). The *Catechism of the Catholic Church* teaches that this evil one is Satan:

> In this petition, evil is not an abstraction, but it refers to a person, Satan, the Evil One, the angel who opposes God. The devil (dia-bolos) is the one who "throws himself across" God's plan and his work of salvation accomplished in Jesus Christ. (*Catechism of the Catholic Church*, 2851)

Evil personified, or Satan, comes from the Hebrew word *Satan*, which means "adversary." Richard McBrien notes that the New Testament "carried over the general Jewish teaching about evil spirits and the devil."[59] Satan, or "the deceiver of the whole world" (John 8:44), is mentioned many times in the New Testament. He is presented as

> ... the "tempter" (Mt. 4:3), the "enemy" (Mt. 13:39; Lk. 10:19), the great dragon (Rev. 12:9, 20:2), the serpent (2 Cor. 11:3), the one who was a murderer and a liar from the beginning (Jn. 8:44; 1 Jn. 3:8), the evil one (Mt. 13:39; Lk. 8: 12; Acts 10:38), Satan (Mk. 3:23, 26, 4:15; Lk. 13:16), Beelzebub (Mt. 12:24, 27; Mk. 3:22; Lk. 11:15, 18, 19), the prince of this world (Jn. 12:31; 2 Cor. 4:4; Eph. 2:2). Simply stated, he is the evil one, the author of lies, of hatred, of sickness, and of death (Mk. 3:23-30; Lk. 13:16; Acts 10:38; Heb. 2:14). Human beings who do not deal justly or love their brothers or sisters (1 Jn. 3:10) are seen to be offspring of the devil, as was Cain (1 Jn. 3:12) and Judas Iscariot (Jn 6:70, 13:2, 27). The tares of Jesus' parable are the children of the evil one, who are opposed to the children of the kingdom (Mt. 13:38)—who *are* the kingdom of God.[60]

The scriptures speak of the existence of the devil. Similarly, official Church teaching continues to speak of the evils of Satan. In one document, we read that Jesus saves us from "the power of darkness and of Satan" (*Ad Gentes*, 3). "When we ask to be delivered from the Evil one, we pray as well to be freed from all evils, present, past and future, of which he is the author or instigator" (*Catechism of the Catholic Church*, 2854). While the scriptures and our tradition affirm the presence of the "Evil One," here we will explore the ways in which we may add to our own sorrow and the sorrow of others through our thoughts, words, and actions. Blaming everything on the evil one takes away from human responsibility, and disbelief in an evil one denies the teaching of our faith. Our tradition explores the many sources of evil.

Deliverance from evil is part of God's plan of salvation. Pope John Paul II makes the connection between salvation and liberation from evil: "To save means to be liberated from radical evil."[61] In this goal to liberate and deliver people from "radical evil," we must choose whether we are going to be an "adversary" of God's kingdom or an "advocate" of God's kingdom. An "adversary" works to destroy, oppress, intimidate, abuse, exploit, shame, enslave, punish, instill fear, and hate God's creatures and creation. An adversary is inspired by evil. An advocate, on the other hand, works to build, support, defend, fulfill, love, encourage, reconcile, heal, forgive, liberate, and deliver God's creatures and creation. An advocate is inspired by love. Unfortunately, several "demons" are often busy trying to prevent us from being advocates: fear, pride, and negative thinking.

Deliverance from fear, pride, and negative thinking

The scriptures challenge us to be fearless in the face of crisis and conflict. Perhaps fear is the last hurdle in this step toward salvation. Conversion and forgiveness may deliver us from pride, but fear may remain. While we may accept that we need help (humility), our fears often try to stifle our desire to be delivered from addiction, abuse, negative emotions, guilt, shame, and oppression. Fear is a universal emotion that gives birth to other negative emotions, such as anxiety. Our preoccupation with unknown results or consequences may prevent us from moving forward. One may find a false sense of security by staying with the familiar, even if the familiar is toxic. In Matthew's gospel, Jesus makes the connection between faith and facing our fears (Matthew 8:23-23, 14:22-33). In these accounts, the presence of Jesus calms the storm, saves the disciples, and reassures Peter. Jesus' actions teach us that we need to choose between fear and love. The fact that Jesus saves people from danger gives all those who are afraid to leave abusive situations, bad work environments, and addictive habits the strength to face their fears. He reminds us that "even the hairs on [our] head[s] are counted" (Matthew 10:30), and that he gives a peace that the world cannot give (John 14:27).

Following Jesus demands that we detach ourselves from all that may harm us. Doing so requires great humility and trust. When a man asked him, "Teacher, what good deed must I do to have eternal life?" (Matthew 19:16), Jesus told the man to keep the commandments. The man said, "I have kept all these; what do I still lack?" (Matthew 19:20) Jesus told him to go and sell his possessions and "give the money to the poor" (Matthew 19:21). The requirement to obey the commandments was followed by an interesting request. The fact that the man was unable to do as Jesus asked tells us that this man was attached to his material possessions. His attachment did not free him up to love God completely. This story has implications for all people who believe they are doing God's will. The last hurdle for them will be to face their fears and detach themselves from anything that enslaves them and prevents freedom. Eternal life with God requires more than just following the law. Deliverance from fear and illusion gives one the courage to step forward in trust.

Deliverance and liberation are not limited to what lies beyond us; we need them within us as well. Human freedom is not merely the result of deliverance from outside forces; it is freedom from the fear within. Jesus came to make this truth known. He speaks of the desire for healing, liberation, and deliverance. To see healing, liberation, and deliverance is to see salvation. Jesus calls us to be positive thinkers (Mark 11:22-24) and to persevere (Luke 11:5-13). The author of Ecclesiastes advises us not to focus on doubt or obsess over unsure futures: "Whoever observes the wind will not sow; and whoever regards the clouds will not reap" (Ecclesiastes 11:4). In other words, if we put things off due to doubt or less than ideal circumstances, we will not reap a harvest of spiritual and material blessings. Hope and trust in God lead us to fulfill God's will. God has a plan for us, but needs us to trust and be positive. Trust in the present brings change in the future.

Dr. Jerome Frank, a former professor of psychiatry at John Hopkins' University School of Medicine, examined many forms of healing as they developed in various social and religious contexts. He was interested in drawing out commonalities and differences. In his study of the process of healing, he noted that one common factor was found in all illnesses: demoralization. He found that those who seek therapy "are conscious of having failed to meet their own expectations or those of others, or of being unable to cope with some pressing problem. They feel powerless to change the situation or themselves …. [t]o various degrees the demoralized person feels isolated, hopeless, and helpless, and is preoccupied with merely trying to survive."[62] Isolation, hopelessness, and helplessness clearly lead to demoralization. Jesus challenges us to hope and love, not fear and despair.

Positive thinking, perseverance, and fearlessness, on the other hand, lead to deliverance. Jesus shows us the way to salvation, as he *is* the way to salvation. Our response to God through faith is made manifest in our repentance, our forgiveness of self and others, and our healing and deliverance from personal and social sin. Christ shows us how to reconcile with God: "God was in Christ reconciling the world, no longer holding humanity's misdeeds against them" (2 Corinthians 5:19). Freedom from sin brings reconciliation. We are called to be "reconciled to God" (2 Corinthians 5:20) and to one another (Matthew 5:24). This call to reconcile, however, may be hard to follow if we are paralyzed by worry.

The Health Consequences of Fear and Negative Thinking

When worry intensifies, the result is fear. At different times in our lives, we may experience fear. A university or college student may feel fear before an exam. A person who has cancer may fear speaking to the oncologist about test results. A teacher may fear discussing student behaviour with parents. A parent may fear that something terrible will happen to his or her child. Often we imagine a negative outcome of an encounter or conversation. Often our fear convinces us that there is no hope. According to Norman Cousins, "[f]ear and panic create negative expectations …. One tends to move in the direction of one's expectations."[63] We may sabotage ourselves with unknown facts or some misguided prediction about the outcome of a given event. This misperception may disturb our peace and move us to believe something that is merely an illusion. Some call this "evil foreboding," that awful feeling that something bad is going to happen. Fear sabotages our peace and tempts us not to trust in God's providence. We may be unable to move forward in hope. With the help of God's grace, our misguided perceptions can be healed. If fear persists, however, it can negatively affect our health. Doctors have documented the health consequences of fear:

> Fear causes the heart to race, the head to spin, the palms to sweat, the knees to buckle, and breathing to become laboured. The level of arousal that results is similar to the effects of stress, and the human body can't withstand it indefinitely.

Fear causes the body to secrete epinephrine, or adrenaline, a hormone also secreted in response to stress. Fear floods the system with epinephrine. Its most powerful effect is on the heart: Both the rate and strength of contractions increase. Blood pressure soars. The body is stimulated to release other hormones, which act on various other organs and systems. In essence, the body is put on alert. If the fear is intense enough, all systems can fatally overload.[64]

The health consequences are clear: fear damages our emotional and physical health. This type of stress may weaken the immune system and cause illness. Positive thinking, on the other hand, can produce life-building results.

Dr. Howard S. Freidman, psychologist and clinical professor of community medicine at the University of California, and Dr. Hans J. Eysenck, have made the connection between personality type and illness.[65] Personality has been defined as "the pattern of behaviour that distinguishes you from everybody else. Personality depends partly on genetics and biology—on the unique set of genes you inherited from your parents—but it is also shaped powerfully by the family you grow up in, the environment that surrounds you, and the culture and subcultures that influence you."[66]

Doctors are now finding that certain personality types may be associated with various illnesses.[67] Yugoslav psychologist Ronald Grossarth-Maticek conducted a famous study. It followed a large number of healthy people over a period of time to determine which personality traits led to disease. It is worth reading a detailed account of this study:

> He started by identifying large random samples of subjects. He recorded each person's current physical health, smoking and drinking habits, and other health behaviours. Then he devised several ways to measure personality, one with a series of short questionnaires, another with lengthy interviews. At the end, Grossarth-Maticek categorized people according to four categories: One was prone to develop cancer; one was prone to develop heart disease; and two who were prone to remain healthy.
>
> He followed each group closely for at least ten years and monitored the people in some groups for thirteen years. The results were remarkable. He was able to predict death from cancer with six times greater accuracy than it was possible to predict based on cigarette smoking.
>
> Among the groups he said were prone to develop cancer (those with a helpless, victimized personality style), almost half *did* die from cancer, but fewer than one in ten died from heart disease. Among those he predicted to be prone to heart disease (those with a hostile, aggressive personality style), more than a third *did* die of heart disease, but only one in five died of cancer.[68]

While many people may question these findings, one useful conclusion we can draw from them is that positive thinking may improve overall quality of life. Anxiety and fear, on the other hand, can disturb one's sense of balance.

"So do not worry about tomorrow, for tomorrow will bring worries of its own. Today's trouble is enough for today" (Matthew 6:34).

In *The Mind and the Brain: Neuroplasticity and the Power of Mental Force,* Dr. Jeffrey M. Schwarz, M.D., and Sharon Begley share their research on the connection between the mind and brain health. They show how "patients could systematically alter their own brain function … and control the very brain chemistry underlying their disease."[69] Dr. Schwarz found that patients who had Obsessive Compulsive Disorder could control their obsessive thoughts by actively focusing their attention away from negative thoughts and toward more positive ones. The result was that patients used this technique to rewire their brains.[70] He applied the same technique to people with dyslexia and people who have had a stroke. He suggests that our own mental force, along with spiritual meditation, can be disciplined to control our thoughts. Imagine how prayer, coupled with this technique, could help people who suffer from chronic worrying.

While healing requires time, patience, discipline, prayer and trust, knowing that we can fulfill Jesus' desire not to worry about tomorrow gives us hope and reassurance. Let us be "of the same mind in the Lord" (Philippians 4:2).

During Lent of 2006, I facilitated two retreats for women. During the retreats, I asked participants to reflect on the importance of fearlessness and positive thinking.

One woman shared a remarkable insight with the group. In her reflection, she pondered the crucifixion and the two thieves crucified with Jesus. She shared that, for her, the two thieves represented her past and future. This was a brilliant insight into the way our shame and bad memories keep us in the past, and how our fear of uncertain outcomes holds us hostage in the future. This woman was right—the past and the future are two thieves who rob us of our peace in the present.

Jesus assured us through his miracles that our faith can make us well (Mark 10:52). While our personalities are determined by genetics, heredity, environment, and other life experiences, God's grace can work with our nature, our choices, and our desire to be made well so that we can face our fears and face the future with hope and positive thinking. Even if our bodies may remain ill, our minds and emotions can be healed so that we have renewed strength and endurance to deal with our struggles. Jesus says, "Have faith in God. Truly I tell you, if you say to this mountain, 'Be taken up and thrown into the sea,' and if you do not doubt in your heart, but believe that what you say will come to pass, it will be done for you. So I tell you, whatever you ask for in prayer, believe that you have received it, and it will be yours" (Mark 11:22-24). Here, Jesus is saying that positive thinking and trust are the keys to our emotional survival.

While I was working to complete my doctorate, I experienced a writer's block that dragged on for three years. This was very humbling; I finally surrendered and was prepared to withdraw from the program. I could not feel God's grace, and interpreted this to mean that I was not called to complete this work. I shared my anxiety with my chiropractor, who said to me, "You must see yourself writing." In other words, I needed to believe that I could write: "believe that you have received it." I did start to believe I could do it, and gradually got back on track with my dissertation.

Fear and worry can prevent us from doing God's will and bringing about our own fulfillment. Trust, love, and gratitude, on the other hand, can lead to restoration. Positive thoughts coupled with God's grace can heal our understanding of ourselves and others. We know a thought by its fruit. If our thoughts lead to anxiety and worry, we must pray for healing as we work to discipline our thoughts. We cannot do it on our own. It is not until we admit our weakness and humility that the light is turned on. We can do all things with Christ who is in us. When I had writer's block, God was showing me that it is God who is working through me. I needed to put my ego and fears aside to make room for God to work.

Pride is another obstacle we must overcome. Pride keeps us focused on ourselves and enslaved to things like perfectionism, attachment to ego, attachment to reputation, and attachment to status. Sometimes, pride is fear of weakness in others and in oneself. In my own life, I have found that for each great accomplishment, several areas of weakness are uncovered. Sanctification is a process that involves uncovering and healing of our weaknesses at a manageable pace—not all at once. God is merciful and will show us the areas of our lives that need healing. Discovering our weaknesses is humbling, but keeps us focused on God's love. Earlier in this book, I mentioned that an ongoing prayer of mine has been not to let affirmation go to my head or criticism get to my heart. When we allow affirmation to go to our heads, we are focused on ourselves. When we allow criticism to get to our hearts, we are focused on ourselves. When our focus is on God, we thank God for our gifts and trust that God will heal our minds and give us understanding.

Honest and sincere correction helps us to move forward, but we must receive it in humility. Attachment to our ego leads us to feel attacked. Jesus corrected many of his followers and critics. Because his critics saw him as attacking them, they responded with attack. Those who were humble, on the other hand, received Jesus' teaching with trust and made a commitment to change their lives.

Abuse is another story. Abuse is not loving correction but soul murder. This type of toxic criticism destroys. Focusing on Jesus and his love for us helps us to see that this type of criticism has nothing to do with us. Rather, someone who is abusive is projecting his or her own fear onto others. Fear leads to feelings of inadequacy, possessiveness, jealousy, and insecurity. At times, a person who fears his or her emotions may in some way blame another for his or her feelings of inadequacy, and this may lead to abuse. Abusive words and actions hurt both the victim and the abuser. Pastoral counselling, psychotherapy, and prayer can help those who have been hurt by abuse. Fear can keep one enslaved to this pain, or inspire the one who inflicts the pain. While it is not within the scope of this book to examine this issue in depth, it is worthwhile to explore the source of this pain. It is God's will that we are delivered from all that prevents authentic human freedom.

Deliverance from the evil of fear, anxiety, and pride are key steps toward salvation:

Deliver us, Lord, we beseech you, from every evil and grant us peace in our day, so that aided by your mercy we might be ever free from sin and protected from all anxiety, as we await the blessed hope and the coming of our saviour, Jesus Christ. (*Roman Missal*, Embolism after the Lord's Prayer, 126)

Reflection questions

- How do you understand evil?
- What is the source of evil?
- How do you deal with fear and negative thinking?

Prayer

God of truth,
help us in our fight against all that is evil.

May we be mindful of any thoughts, deeds, and words
that may frustrate your will for us.

Grant that we have the wisdom to know the difference
between good and evil.

Show us how to feel, see, and speak truth.

We ask this through Christ our Lord.

Amen.

Amen
(So be it!)

W hile one short book cannot exhaust the mystery of salvation, salvation for me remains multi-dimensional. It is worldly and otherworldly, personal and communal, and communicates God's great love for creation. Understanding salvation as the fulfillment of the Lord's Prayer in this world and in the next addresses the physical, spiritual, and universal needs of individuals and communities. Understood this way, salvation relates to men and women of all races, classes, cultures, and religions. For eleven years I have looked to various sources to find the meaning of salvation—Scripture, the official documents of the Church, classical and contemporary theology, early Christian writers, the mystics. Each of these sources, coupled with my own faith and lived experience, has informed my understanding of salvation.

My view of salvation continues to be connected to Jesus Christ. "Jesus means in Hebrew: 'God saves.' At the annunciation, the angel Gabriel gave him the name Jesus as his proper name, which expresses both his identity and his mission to save his people from their sins'" (*Catechism of the Catholic Church*, 430, p. 96; see also Matthew 1:21). For those who believe in God, their image of God may determine their world view. Christians are called to view God through Jesus: "He is the image of the invisible God, the firstborn of all creation ..." (Colossians 1:15). Jesus says, "Whoever has seen me has seen the Father. Do you not believe that I am in the Father and the Father is in me?" (John 14:9). Jesus gives us an insight into how God loves God's creation. By learning about Jesus Christ, we learn how God feels about those who suffer, those who need forgiveness, and those who need healing. While Jesus Christ is the way of salvation, the Lord's Prayer provides the instruction manual or map for this "way." Christians are blessed with a tour guide who drew the map: Jesus Christ. We also have another advocate who helps us along this journey: the Holy Spirit. The Holy Spirit continues God's work to save all people. The Spirit helps people to be brought to holiness and be made well. The Spirit helps us to fulfill the petitions of the Lord's Prayer in our daily lives. The Holy Spirit sanctifies us and leads us to health and fulfillment. God the Father parents us through the work of Jesus Christ and the action of the Holy Spirit.

So the question remains: Can the Lord's Prayer assist Christians in their study and reflection of what it means to be saved? I believe the answer is yes. Christians are called to be signs of salvation for the world. Our witness serves as a tribute to Jesus Christ, who shows us the way to salvation, for he is "the way and the truth and the life" (John 14:6). He makes the journey easier, since his "yoke is easy" and his "burden is light" (Matthew 11:30). Through baptism, Christians have been lit by God's grace: "No one after lighting a lamp puts it in a cellar, but on the lamp stand so that those who enter may see the light" (Luke 11:33). The official teaching of the Church is that salvation is accomplished in Jesus Christ and completed in the Body of Christ through the work of the Holy Spirit. The fulfillment of the Lord's Prayer in the Body of Christ will serve to bring about the completion of salvation. Thus, when we fulfill the Lord's Prayer in our communities, we will help to liberate and inspire others.

The Lord's Prayer offers hope and consolation to those in need. A person may be suffering due to poverty, an abusive spouse, or a child who has an addiction. Does this person need to be fed, clothed, and sheltered: "Give us this day our daily bread"? Does this person need to be delivered from evil: "rescue us from the evil one"? Does this person need assistance in his or her "time of trial"? Does he or she seek God's will "on earth as it is in heaven"? Do his or her spouse and children need deliverance from sin and weakness? And do not all need forgiveness from themselves, others, and God? Only by following God's will can we find true fulfillment and comfort, for following God's will brings grace or divine assistance. We know a tree by its fruit. Ignoring God's will leads to pain, guilt, disappointment, and fear. The gifts and fruits of the Holy Spirit are the key to growth. The gifts of the Holy Spirit are our weapons against enslavement, and the fruits of the Holy Spirit are the result of using these gifts. God's will calls for us to use these gifts as they lead us to bear fruit in our lives.

Jesus knew salvation. He lived salvation and is salvation (Luke 2:29-32). Our challenge is to understand more fully this gift that God desires to give, and to share in a discussion of the fulfillment that many people desire—a fulfillment that has been described, preached, and revealed in Jesus Christ. Salvation, as Jesus understood and taught it, has universal and inclusive meaning. It is a gift and a life-giving process that leads to fulfillment in this life and the next, for all people and for all time. A deeper understanding of salvation will be enriching for all faithful people who seek the truth. Seminarians, lay students of theology, clergy, lay ministers, theologians, and religious educators will find that a more solid grasp of the meaning of salvation will help them in their work. In interreligious dialogue, such knowledge can help us explain our understanding of salvation and how it is connected to Jesus Christ. We will not be limited to the realm of mystery; rather, we can discuss what salvation means for us.

Our faith should transform us, but transformation takes time. We are called to be patient with ourselves and others. God's plan unfolds in small doses, with teachings and lessons we can receive when we are ready. Over the past ten years, one of my prayers has been this: "Lord, help me to see truth, feel truth, and speak truth." God helps us to see ourselves as we are, and Jesus helps us to see ourselves as we should be: saved and free.

Pray, then, in this way:

Our Father in heaven, hear our cry for salvation.

Hallowed be your name; may we always remember to praise you.

Your kingdom come so that we may be fulfilled.

Your will be done, not mine, **on earth as it is in heaven.**

Give us this day our daily bread so that our basic human needs can be met.

And forgive us our debts, as we also have forgiven our debtors, so that we can be made well.

And do not bring us to the time of trial so that we can resist unfulfilling habits and thoughts.

But rescue us from the evil one so that we may be free to love, without fear, pride, or anxiety.

Amen.

Endnotes

1   Augustine of Hippo, Ep. 130, 12, 22: PL 33, 503.

2   Thomas Aquinas, STh. II–II, 83, 9.

3   Leonardo Boff, *The Lord's Prayer: The Prayer of Integral Liberation* (Maryknoll, NY: Orbis Books, 1983), 4.

4   Boff, *The Lord's Prayer*, 6.

5   Boff, *The Lord's Prayer*, 18.

6   Boff, *The Lord's Prayer*, 18.

7   See Joachim Jeremias, *Abba: The Prayers of Jesus* (Philadelphia: Fortress Press, 1978), 89.

8   Boff, *The Lord's Prayer*, 19.

9   There are now nineteen blessings, as one has been added.

10 Didache 8.

11 Greg Anderson, *Cancer and the Lord's Prayer: Hope and Healing Through History's Greatest Prayer* (Des Moines, IO: Jordan House, 2006), 25.

12 Boff, *The Lord's Prayer*, 33.

13 Statistics Canada Study, completed 1994–1995. See statcan. gc.ca.

14 See www.statcan.gc.ca.

15 Boff, *The Lord's Prayer*, 32.

16 Peter Chrysologus, Sermo 71, 4: PL 52:402A; cf. Rom. 2:24; Ezek. 36:20-22.

17 Boff, *The Lord's Prayer*, 58.

18 Thich Nhat Hanh, *Living Buddha, Living Christ* (New York: Riverhead Books, 1995), 38.

19 For an exegetical analysis of "this day" see Boff, *The Lord's Prayer*, 78–80.

20 UN Human Development Report, 2009: http://hdr.undp.org/ en.

21 UN report: "The Relationship Between Disarmament and Development in the Current International Context." 59th Session of UN General Assembly, September 2004. www.un.org/en/index.shtml.

22 Statistics adapted from *On Any Given Night: Measuring Homelessness in Hamilton.* Hamilton Community Services, City of Hamilton, 2006.

23 See Psalm 7:11; 18:28; 22:22; 34:7; Isaiah 12:2, 35; Exodus 15:2.

24 See Acts 27:18-20; Luke 6:20f; Romans 6f; 1 Timothy 1:15; Ephesians 2:1-10.

25 UN Human Development Report, 2009 http://hdr.undp.org/en/.

26 See Canadian Conference of Catholic Bishops, *Do Justice! The Social Teaching of the Canadian Catholic Bishops.* Ed. E.F. Sheridan, S.J. (Toronto: Éditions Paulines and the Jesuit Centre for Social Faith and Justice, 1987).

27 Canadian Conference of Catholic Bishops, "Labour Day Message," 1971, 209.

28 *The Cloud of Unknowing*, trans. Ira Progroff (New York: Julian Press, 1969), 94.

29 M. T. Morter, *The Soul Purpose* (Arkansas: Dynamic Life, 2001) 108.

30 See Leo Thomas, O.P., and Jan Alkire, *Healing as a Parish Ministry: Mending Body, Mind, and Spirit* (Notre Dame, IN: Ave Maria Press, 1992), 39.

31 See James P. Henry, "The Arousal of Emotions: Hormones, Behaviour, and Health," *Advances*, 6: 2, 59–62.

32 See Brent Q. Hafen, Keith J. Karren, Kathyrn J. Frandsen, N. Lee Smith, M.D., *Mind/Body Health: The Effects of Attitudes, Emotions, and Relationships* (Boston: Allynt Bacon, 1996), 21.

33 Dr. Robert Ader is director of the division of behavioural and psychosocial medicine at New York's University of Rochester.

34   Hafen et al., *Mind/Body Health*, 21.

35   Hafen et al., *Mind/Body Health*, 23.

36   Hafen et al., *Mind/Body Health*, 25.

37   Hafen et al., *Mind/Body Health*, 390.

38   Joan Borysenko, *Minding the Body, Mending the Mind* (Reading, MA: Addison-Wesley, 1987), 176.

39   See Dan Custer, *The Miracle of Mind Power* (Englewood Cliffs, NJ: Prentice-Hall, 1960).

40   Hafen et al., *Mind/Body Health*, 391. See also Robin Casarjian, "Forgiveness: An Essential Component in Health and Healing," in Proceedings of the Fourth National Conference on the Psychology of Health, Immunity, and Disease, published by the National Institute for the Clinical Application of Behavioural Medicine.

41   Anderson, *Cancer and the Lord's Prayer*, 37.

42   *Healing as a Parish Ministry,* 17, 44.

43   Francis S. Collins, *A Scientist Presents Evidence for Belief: The Language of God* (New York: Free Press, 2006), 230.

44   U.S. Census Bureau Statistics: www.census.gov.

45   Drug and Rehabilitation Services in the U.S.: see www.drugandalcoholrehab.net.

46   See www.statcan.gc.ca.

47   Collins, *A Scientist Presents Evidence for Belief*, 263.

48   See Gerald May, *Addiction and Grace* (San Francisco: HarperSanFrancisco, 1988).

49   May, *Addiction and Grace*, 14.

50   May, *Addiction and Grace*, see 26–31.

51   See Jay Ingram, "How Addictions Change the Brain." *Hamilton Spectator.* Friday, January 14, 2005.

52   May, *Addiction and Grace,* 60.

53   May, *Addiction and Grace*, 16.

54   May, *Addiction and Grace*, 90.

55   May, *Addiction and Grace*, 90.

56 May, *Addiction and Grace*, 92.

57 Meissner, *Psychology of a Saint,* 88.

58 Ratzinger, "Commentary on *Gaudium et Spes,"* 160.

59 Richard McBrien, *Catholicism,* 343.

60 Boff, *The Lord's Prayer*, 112–113.

61 John Paul II, *Crossing the Threshold of Hope,* 67.

62 Jerome Frank, *Persuasion and Healing* (New York: Schocken Books, 1973), 314. See also Jerome Frank, "The Role of Hope in Psychotherapy," *International Journal of Psychiatry*: Vol. 5 (1968), 383–95. See also Paul Preyser, "The Phenomenology and Dynamics of Hoping." *The Journal of the Scientific Study of Religion*: Vol. 3 (1963), 93–94.

63 Norman Cousins, *The Healing Heart* (New York: W. W. Norton, 1983).

64 Hafen et al., *Mind/Body Health,* 211.

65 See Howard S. Friedman, *The Self-Healing Personality* (New York: Henry Holt and Company, 1991). Also Hans J. Esyneck, "Health's Character," *Psychology Today,* December 1988, and "Personality, Stress, and Cancer: Prediction and Prophylaxis," *British Journal of Medical Psychology* (part 1), 61: 1988, 57–75.

66 Hafen et al., *Mind/Body Health,* 97.

67 Hafen et al., *Mind/Body Health,* 97.

68 Hafen et al., *Mind/Body Health,* 98–99.

69 Jeffrey M. Schwartz and Sharon Begley, *The Mind and The Brain: Neuroplasticity and the Power of Mental Force* (New York: HarperCollins, 2002), 7.

70 Please note that I offer an oversimplification of the technique. I am a theologian, not a scientist; therefore, interested readers are encouraged to read the book to discover the details of the technique used.